I0410186

the
funny
fight

by martin bector

© 2002 by Martin Bector. All rights reserved.

No part of this book may be reproduced, stored in a retrieval system, or
transmitted by any means, electronic, mechanical, photocopying, recording,
or otherwise, without written permission from the author.

ISBN: 1-4033-6091-X (e-book)
ISBN: 1-4033-6092-8 (Paperback)

This book is printed on acid free paper.

1stBooks – rev. 01/08/03

TABLE OF CONTENTS

CHAPTER I – Part I

I have begun a fight with President George W. Bush Jr. at the beginning of his first term in office as President of the United States of America. This is a funny fight.

I have solved the mind, the psychology, the recall and the will. The Oval Office is the prize. The fight is a funny fight because the fight in the Light is not the same fight as in the Darkness.

I have begun this fight because I want to bring to the people in the United States of America, all the people on this side of this earth and all the people on the other side of earth a new freedom.

Freedom came not from the work of the people on this earth to build as it is in Heaven on this Earth. Freedom came from an escape. The reaching to the land on this earth from the other side of earth became not freedom for the people on this side of earth.

The fight of the people on this land and on this side of earth has reached about the spirit of America and captured the face of this side of earth. The spirit of the Oval Office is the heart of America. The spirit is the love of God. The mind is awakened in the spirit. The awakening brings the mind to be the Love of God.

I am not religious. I believe prayer is the same sin as the reason a little creature dies to feed a big creature as its prey. I have put this curiosity beside the state in the separation of the Church and State. I recognize the little creature has to run and hide to escape the danger. I see the survival of the creature in a course on this earth. I look at the people coming to this side of this earth. I look at the people from the beginning on this land to the present.

I see the people have accepted the coming of God in the Light. I have read the Holy Bible. I have gone to school. I recognize the coming of God in the Darkness is foretold to begin at the End Time of the year 2000. I immediately see myself as the one foretold to bring the meeting of the Light and Darkness. No other is on this earth about the coming of God in the view of Darkness.

I call this a funny fight, this meeting of the Light and Darkness, because the people on earth do not know that the Light is the sight before the eyes and the Darkness is the sight inside the head. The people on this earth are expecting the meeting to be people meeting people.

I want to bring you to see the truth as I see the truth. You in the leadership of the United States of America and on this side of earth became who you are by a fight. How can I stand beside you unless I come by the

1

same fight? My right hand does not tear off my left hand. My right eye does not lie to my left eye. I walk in a straight line. My feet are not in this tangle about the two sides of my body.

The meeting of the sight of the eyes is a focus. This is the real guide to freedom. The ability of the hands to continue the same activity making the work easier is the practice of freedom. The steps made by the feet are the way of freedom. Mankind is made in the image of God. The image came on this earth and the presence of mankind began to interpret the image. The interpretation of the image is what mankind taught on this earth.

I am aware of one interpretation of the image and President George W. Bush Jr. is aware of another interpretation of the image. The meeting of the two interpretations has become the funny fight. The fight is funny because in the long run, there is only one image all the people of earth are aware of from the Alpha to the Omega.

There was only one God in the beginning. The many gods knowing gods and this earth are directions. God gave the many gods the truth from the beginning to eternity before the coming of mankind to earth. The many gods can only repeat the truth put by God bringing the many gods to be directions. God did this in the beginning, when all the gods were presenting their power and love to God as gifts to help God bring about relativity to the presence of all that is on this earth. The people all come from God. The many different distinctions and the senses determining the difference between things on this earth are relative to the seasons on this earth. This Universe is an expanding universe. The reaching out by the presence of God is by this expansion.

The absence of this direction from the god's God depends on is called denial. The people are being lead to believe the people's denial is denying God. This is not true. The denial to God is impossible. God put the truth all the way to eternity.

The first has to put a relationship for the second and the second has to form the same obedience to regulate the progress going both ways. The progress going both ways is the same. Bringing an identical witness is this relativity. The Theory of Relativity can put the Atomic Theory in words. Adding the people is the 6-66 formula, once the numbers and the letters are about the gathering. The adding of the people brings the sound into this addition. The addition of the sound is the next revelation.

The New Testament Revelation written in the Holy Bible foretells the gathering of the number and the letter. The truth in the coming of God revealed in the view of the Darkness knows the revelation's beginning as foretold in the New Testament Revelation and the many revelations to follow. The sound is the awakening to be with the people followed by the color, the color code, the speed, the form and the image.

The End Time of the year 2000 is upon this earth. I have begun to stand up, as is prophesized. There were no white people, black people or oriental people on this side of earth before the people came to this side in big boats. I have awakened the Light and the Darkness each separately and together to be with the Brilliance, the Light, the Darkness and the Blackness by my turning the reaching about this earth back and forth. I worked this system until the answers came with a foundation. I recognized that I could not remember the perfect answers reaching to me because I had no foundation for the answers. The image has been replaced on this earth about the education by the identity. The identity has been in a wilderness. The objective of a wilderness is survival. Progress has a more far-reaching objective.

The funny fight is in the psychology because the one the government is using between me and the Oval office has deceased. I have stood up to claim all that should have been mine. The sight of the Oval office cannot be hidden behind the confusion any more. All that has transpired on this earth is awaken to a new world as it was foretold in the New Testament Revelation. The people who interpreted the New Testament Revelation put the recognition back by the identity to the past. The end of the world is really the beginning answers to a new world.

I bring this same fight public. The fight is the death of the world verses the harvest of the world. The end of the year is a harvest time. Jesus told the truth. Jesus said, "put it public". Look at the name Adam. The name Adam has been taken personally to be the name of a man. The story of the name Adam and the sin of Adam are recognized all around this earth. The obedience to Jesus has been denied. I obeyed Jesus and Jesus put me to an awareness revealing the name Adam put public means to add the AM. The name Adam is a command and a commandment.

The new world bringing about the End Time of the present world has been received and written. The new world is to be built by a new government designed to the sun inside out. I have been instructed to bring the blessings to be the answers by solving the mysteries of God. I have received and written the answers to build the new government designed to the sun inside out.

I want you to be aware that I have also been given instructions to build the End Time for the present world built by the present government. This building of the End Time coming to this earth as foretold in the New Testament Revelation brings about the sight of the End Time to be a wall to the next step as the End Time. The End Time has to be built on this earth. This wall is the necessity enabling the people to rise up to the salvation.

I know you will not understand what, I'm telling, so I have put this in writing. You are being lead to your obedience by the power sound of the

3

word meeting the interpretation of the image. Not having the meeting by the number and the letter as a foundation puts President George W. Bush Jr. at the same disadvantage I began with as a child. The present government will have to build the End Time in order to rise up the people. The funny fight gets real funny as the top and bottom begins to majority rule the Republicans and Democrats by swishing back and forth the white people and the black people. The back and forth movement is better noticed by the movement of the Light and the Darkness being the sight before the eyes and the sight inside the head.

I plan to put the answers before some people bringing the way to be the destiny for a few. My people and the President's people are not the fight between the good and the bad as the preachers are persuading the people. Good and better are coming from the New Testament Revelation turned to go the right way.

I don't want the religions to hand over in a game of keep-away the truth from the top or bottom as a way of control. I want what I reveal not to be a religion or a government or a society at the beginning. I want this to be a profitable business. I am in possession of the answers to building the new government. The present governments on this earth have been prepared for the coming of this new government designed to the sun inside out. The awareness to the reaching of my new government is prepared to use the present governments as a foundation eliminating any misuse or mistrust between the people. It is not a government that is beyond the government. Beyond the government is another way by harmony. Government is by control, it is not a government that is beyond the government.

The funny fight is at the top. The fight at the bottom is a real fight because the reaching of the truth from God comes with the children. The same insult which forced me away from my land and my future is this being wrapped around the children causing the children to be insulted. Nativity is not this measure by the law coming with and from the United States government. I have no intention of bringing this understanding to be used against the blond people, the black people or any person. Keep the government whole.

The bottom tells on the top. The police keep this hidden in an effort to try to make a place for the people on this earth intending to replace the End Time wall. The recognition of the lawyers and the law bring the police to reveal the course of the law to control the people. Recognizing that harmony and control go in the opposite direction, the police need to become the End Time wall or they will be replaced by the coming of the force able to rise up the people. In the truth the government cannot make the police the End Time because God put the truth all the way to eternity. The government and the law cannot be recognized as eternal.

4

Look at the empires being overcome by the kingdoms and the kingdoms being overcome by the governments. The next step to the government has begun at the End Time of the year 2000 as foretold in the Holy Bible. The funny fight becomes as obvious as a clown, as the government of the United States of America tries to deny God and remain the height of the progress about gathering on this earth.

The reaching beyond the government is being forced to the side and only allowed to seep into the cracks at the bottom. The people trying to organize the cracks at the bottom are recognized as corruption. The government loses control at the turn. The straight way is the awareness to society. The turns are about survival at the bottom. The turn at the top is called a race. The reaching of the force will bring the turn from the race to the pace.

The bottom reaching up to the top brings the practice of legislation to be sophisticated enough to appear as the answers for the bottom and as a new recognition able to stand beside religion. I am to do no more at this point of the legislation than to bring awareness to the people on this earth.

The meeting of the bottom and the top is not as is expected. The becoming of the top to be with a two-party system is seen and this becoming brings the two-party system to be like a strand of barbwire. The bottom forming a two-party system brings about the actuality of a barbwire fence with more than one strand of barbwire. The meeting is at the fence pole.

The awakening to the fence pole has been called the linage of Adam. This awareness taken to the other side of this earth is called the return of God. I know your mind is as active as mine. I went to the same schools as you. I had the opportunity to read the same books as you read. We speak the same language. It took me forty years to put this inside my head. I cannot expect you to activate the responses at the first reading. The reason I am not with the mind of the people in education is because I had to beg the teacher for a "D" to graduate from high school. The best people are put in course of progress. The worst are left to the forces of survival. My awakening from the forces of survival to the presence of progress is the reason I am called the beast in the writings of the New Testament Revelation.

The first of nativity was put about the people as the first born. The recognition to nativity is the new born. By my education standard and the standard by the selection the present government in the United States of America, I have found it more fun to be about a dance hall than a military armory in the psychology. The street presence has not yet learned to kick up its heels.

The people on this earth have accepted only the coming of God in the view of the light. The darkness has been called evil. The coming of God seen in the darkness brings the same answers as the coming of God in the view of the light. The presence of God is by addition from the beginning. This is revealed in the name Adam meaning to add the AM. The sight before the eyes reveals the rewards God put on this earth in the beginning.

The awakening to the sight inside the head is the darkness. The people on this earth have tried to bring the night time and the day time to be this awareness becoming as the light and the darkness. The name Adpm is the addition of the PM. The name Adpm awakens the awareness to the sight inside the head. The meeting of the sight before the eyes and the sight inside the head has been called the Armageddon. The confusion puts the coming of God in the view of the light to be in a fight with the coming of God in the view of darkness.

The top has been with the name Adam. The bottom has been with the name Devil. My bringing the name Adpm to the public will turn the attention of the people at the evening horizon to be able to recognize the morning horizon to be the same command and commandment put with the name Adam. The turn at the right place does not send the people to hell. The turn brings the people the advantage now lost. The people on this earth have been forced to live in less than half a world.

If you are not laughing at the funny fight by the time you have read about this awakening, it is only because the pain and the hurt do not let the laughter address the mind about your personal interest. There is so much that you do not know. You are trying to put your mind to the end of your life. The New Testament Revelation tells the people to learn to put their mind to the year. The end of your life is too much for your mind to grasp to bring about the obedience needed to obey God.

The End Time of the year 2000 has been foretold. The people on this earth have been prepared for the End Time of the year 2000. The beginning of the year 2000 presented the answers to build the world of God. The last part of the year 2000 presented to me the obedience to complete the answers to build the world of God. I wrote the answers and the obedience. Receiving the answers set God free. Writing the answers set the spirit and the deep free. Completing the answers sets the soul free. The people are put on this earth to complete the answers. The glory must go to God, so God can prepare and send the next step. God returning is this next step. The continuing around this earth becomes this return of God every 2000 years.

I am interested in learning the seasons of the galaxy and putting a comparison to the seasons of the universe and the seasons of this earth. I have solved the reaching from the life beyond this earth to and from the sun. I found the sun to be a door in the psychology. I recognize this in the psychology called Ying and Yang to be this earth, as the day and night at the mind sight telling this earth turns around its axis.

6

I can open this door for you. I first must teach you to be good all the time at the flesh and in the psychology. Once you have mastered the art of being good, I will bring you to learn to put your mind to the Oval office. Learn this ability and I will teach you to turn from seeking God to learn to receive from God. The secret is to recognize the awareness presented from beyond this earth reaching to the sun passing this earth coming and going.

The door has been this insult called voices in the head. The valence of the children has been awakened to the fact that the answers of the children are not the love of the children. The moment the children realize the answers and the love are being insulted in order to attempt to steal the children's future called living through your children, parental sibling rivalry appears.

The simple fact of bringing the children to look at the print of their hand can put an end to the rivalry. The sight is this that has been over run by the police in an attempt to control the people. Combating this error brings the force to replace the police.

The coming of a brand new world coming to replace the present world awakened all at once has been this expectation. This can be. The gathering of the people to bring about all that has been built has been tremendous. This becoming is similar to busy bees building a beehive. What bee tells which bees to follow to begin building a new beehive? Which pigeon is the pigeon telling the flock of pigeons when to fly?

I have received this answer pertaining to people. The answer came as the steps to the entrance to the way of God. The steps in the way of God are Gathering, Measuring, Employment and Freedom. The levels to the entrance to the way of God are registration, subscription, gathering and separation. The meetings of the preparation for the entrance to the way of God and the way of God meet at the gathering. The separation is about direction, not another God or another way of Life.

I want to open your heart to the love of God. I want not to take you away from your religion or your government. My telling you about building the End Time and building the new world is similar to the preparation for the entrance to the way of God. I must bring you to complete the present government, so you will be happy and feel good about the present government. The new government is the future not called a government.

The present Government in the United States goes from the top down. The top turns into a vicious circle. This is the reason the top depends on the mafia. The mafia has been stopping the vicious circle. The black people are aware of this and are casting the black gangs to work for the black people in the same awareness. It is better to complete the government from the bottom up. The commandment of God is to rise up the people. Rising up the people can be done at the same time as completing the government. The

New Testament Revelation tells this practice to become the gathering of the numbers and the letters. Tax dollar is the number. The record is the letter. Giving the credit to the word of God puts the direction to be this awareness bringing all the directions to take a turn in this harmony revealed by God.

The war in Heaven has been solved. The people trying to go back to God are in a fight with the new life trying to come to this earth. Hell has been the fight with the new life of the creatures. The turn to go the other way was to learn to love God through Jesus. I bring another turn bringing the people to obey God.

I have brought you through the mysteries of God by what I have put in writing to bring public the awareness that has been secret on this earth. I now awaken you to the mind of this earth. The mind is the love of God. The people on this earth have been trying to live in the brain. The turn from the presence of the people trying to be aware of God to the people knowing the truth has been called the salvation.

CHAPTER II – Part II

I want to make you aware that if you read past this sentence you have entered into a different world than you are used to living in. The brain is divided into two parts. One part is the personal mind. The other part is the public mind. Jesus called the public mind as the world. The presence to the one side or the other of the brain bringing about the personal or the public awareness is not by your doing. This is a mystery I have yet to understand.

The personal mind is focused to the print on your hands, body and feet. The public mind is this awareness about the presence from the Brilliant Stars to the Black Holes. I first awaken you to the reaching to be about the sun by the sun's eruptions and the black spots on the sun. The Brilliant Stars and the Black Holes know this on this earth. The passage beyond the door I open for you can be more than you are ready to address.

I became the devil himself the first time I entered the door. I learned about his door from hell. I have yet to hear anyone tell that they have learned about this door from heaven. Heaven and hell are both this being before life and after life. You practice on this earth the thing you intend to do for the rest of your time. Death is such a long time. Being dead for so long brings the dead to wish to be reborn. This wish is fruitless. Do not feel sorry for them. They have had theirs. Tell them to share what they learned with the living and know the continuing of God is the presence on this earth.

I came about this by a horrible fight with death. I was hurled to the floor at the age of six months to be admitted to the first 6 in 666. Many people die and go to heaven in the moments of death. Some win the fight and come back to life. I went to hell. I became with the second six as I beat death. I was thrown out of a speeding car at the age of three. I won the fight in hell against death. From hell I awoke to bring the darkness out of the evil.

It was not necessary for me to be at the door of death. The brain concussion only put away the awareness in segments, until I was able to bring the awakening to be on paper, so I could arrange the moments to be free and in the right places. The damage had let the society put the reaching from the Oval office to others by their competition.

The black people called this way of trying to steal my future at the same time as stealing my land the only game in town. The white people called this free ride as the game people played. The freedom in the United States came to get sicker and sicker, until the game returned to where it started, at the mindless. The people in the old world have been practicing on the mindlessness of the retarded and have put the mindlessness in this height of government. The mindlessness has not the sense to tell the truth. Bringing no objection was the public will.

I want to bring you to be aware of the reason the reaching is starting in the north as foretold in the New Testament Revelation. The continuing of God from the east around this earth comes to continue in the turning of this earth around its axis and around this solar system. The charting of the continuing beginning in the east will wrap around this earth for another 2000 years and bring again the return of God from another direction in the year 4000.

The direction and the wrapping can be charted by knowing the point of the east, the point of the north and the turning of this earth about its axis. This chart is more valuable than the wealth on this earth. The last 2000 years should have had this chart.

The meeting of the four directions, by a recording brings the chart to be the written word. The memory will awaken the people at each direction bringing the meeting into a new world. The presence of the four new awakenings is that the people can recognize the coming of God to this earth as an addition called by the names Adam and Adpm.

By my understanding, you can see why I laugh at the funny fight. I really did become the devil. I really did escape from hell. I was put into hell because many people do not resist the persuasion telling that I have no soul. I am aware of this side of earth like they are aware of the other side of earth. The awareness bringing the rewards that God put from the beginning on this earth to complete the answers is called the soul. Legislation can be this awareness in the steps of the way of God. Legislation can begin and stand by the side of religion. Can you imagine having two sides to the street in the way of God?

Do you know the difference between hunger and thirst? Look at this similarity between the awareness, religion and the new sophisticated legislation rising up beside religion in the separation of Church and State. Add the people similar to the formula 6-66 in the third revelation being sound. This similarity will eliminate the repetition and bring the progress to go faster. The new world orchestrates this advantage and brings the sale of this knowledge to become a profit from the prophecy. The actual progress is another profit. Correction and redirection are another profit. The way of legislation is closer to business than to religion by being a profit basis in this wringing out of religion to continue in the truth with God.

I am called the anti Christ because I bring a turn from the non-profit to the profit. Giving away money to a profit business has high tax revenue. This turn of the tax is no more than twice the tax amount. Beyond this tax amount the new legislation actively puts the activity bringing about the proper changes to a growing nation. Money is a record and no more the root of all evil.

Profit and non-profit are the reason there is a gap between rich and poor. It is not best to eliminate one. It is best to bring the possibilities of the two to be side by side to balance the matter and the flow of money. This awareness will bring the necessity for the blinds of Lady Justice to come off. She must begin to see the turn of the law and bring about the fold of the law. The people on this land have run out of wilderness. The rising up of the people side by side to the advances should as well begin at the bottom as the top. Starting at the bottom is the only way the bottom can rise up.

The funny fight between President George W. Bush and I starts by your putting this writing to his awareness. I feel that it should be that the first to reach the President of every nation should be rewarded. Look at the way of this reward and by choosing another to responsibly give you a reward for bringing the contents of this writing to their attention, you can get extra money paying you to buy this little book.

I want to bring it public, the conversation, the time, the date and the amount of the reward. Tell me and I will give you a reward if they fail to reward you or add to the present reward. The whole activity to reach this personality can be recorded and published to awaken another reward from the sleep of not knowing. Awaken this activity as an ambition and keep perfect records. Simply record the activity at the moment of the activity.

The price of this book accumulated to one hub gives you credit. You receive a copy of my book for a price and the price becomes a cost/credit awakened at your will. The $25 price pays for the registration fee to the loan. Pay this fee happily and you are eligible to receive a $200 loan at the 12th participation paying $25 as a registration fee. You can pay the loan with a $5 commission I give for bringing about the sale of my writing. The loan is made for the completion of the answers building the new world.

Pay the first loan and receive immediately a $2000 loan at the 12th participation world wide paying their $200 loan. Pay the second loan and immediately receive a $20,000 loan at the 12th participation world wide paying their loan. This formula can reach fascinating sums able to build entire cities. God personally appeared to me and put this formula to be on this earth with the answers and the way to gather the money to build the city of God on this earth.

The registration level is this coming from the registration fee. The subscription fee awakens the second level delivering the Miracle Commission. The first two levels each can take an entire university to parade the entire possibilities coming from the first two steps meeting, similar to the meeting of the Light and the Darkness. This meeting has been put with the day and the night. This error has brought the people to remain

11

in the creature's world. The day and night begin to concern the creatures first because the creatures were put on this earth before the coming of mankind. Natural is this recognition. Survival is the first world.

The next level gathering has a fascination delivering the way of the first two levels by keeping the profit margin. The addition of the pledge not involving exchange of money, until the gathering allows the use of a Cain letter and a new system and a Star of David to awaken to the fourth level bringing a direction to the people participating.

The money can be recorded to another new system by one dollar and this matching of your dollar; you are eligible to receive $1,000,000 for each 1,000,000 participations. The use of this new system and the Cain letter have been with the actual money exchange putting the Star of David to be lost to religion. I found the star of the Jewish Religion. I saw to put numbers and letters together. I am sure nations will get involved in this formula 6-66 at the level of separation after the gathering in the entrance to the way of God because the 666 is a formula of thought. Direction is this place best to recognize the reaching of the people participating in this blessing bringing the answers by awareness, receiving, writing and intending to complete the answers.

It is foretold that I am bringing the Darkness to be a religion awakening in the Mideast beginning the Armageddon. It is this awareness that the black people have tried to bring as their awareness. The black people are trying to follow the white people. The present blond people are white. The blond people have been commanded to begin a reach from the civilian side of Nellis Air Force Base at the main gate all the way to Northern Canada and build a kingdom for the blond God. This command is not understood.

Africa has awakened the sight from the tip of Africa to the center of the Cross in the Mideast. The sand has put the same, as the ocean, to bring the cleaning similar to the cleaning of the water from the ocean through the mountain streams. The people do not want to mess with voo doo at the sophistication of the awareness. The past is not alive and the opening in the eyes put the spell not to be with words. The spell cannot exit beyond the opening of the eyes and brings the Armageddon to become the arm of Geddon. The continuing around this earth will awaken this force as many times as necessary to be with the wrist of Geddon as the Oval office. The reach to awaken Africa is calling the people to Africa from England, and then continuing around this earth.

By this that appears to me, I know that your children's children will read this writing. This beginning in the darkest part of Africa can be seen all around this earth by a communication. The communication awakens this sudden step to be about all people in all nations by invitation. The sight is able to employ both ways. The freedom has not come with this two-way communication because the law has not kept with the progress.

God put the waiting to be one way being the same way as the turn of this earth about its axis. The reaching by the return of God was foretold to be on this earth beginning at the End Time of the year 2000. This gathering is about the freedom. The gathering going the other way beginning at the gathering is to meet the same place at the center of the Cross by a registration to an invitation.

Every form of business can be put with this invitation to a like mind gathering. I intend to put into a website all the records from gatherings of Government, Law, Religion, Society and Business bringing about a census eliminating the struggle of the government. This report will bring the government to look at the people as a number and a letter and bring free the steps beyond the Government, Law, Religion and Society as a business bringing the revelation of opinion as the salvation including people by their ability.

The race is backwards bringing the finish line to be the equality. The equality should be the starting line to be a real race. The answer to bring about the pace is this End Time of the race for a short time. I see no reason to wait. I want to include the answers to the pace in the delivery at the same price as the answers to build the new world starting by building the new government designed to the sun inside out. Blending the delivery to the new world and the pace at the same time can bring a record census worth a lot of money to each nation.

The answers to the correction of the present course of the present governments on this earth will bring to me a large amount of money from every nation on this earth. I will give credit and I am interested in owning a mountain in every nation on this earth. This is not including the answers to complete the present governments to reach from the top down and from the bottom up. This series of answers will cost the governments another large sum of money.

The funny fight will make me very proud. I have been the wooden nickel rolling with the tumbling tumbleweeds. I began to notice the wind was trying to make me happy, when I was sad. I saw the little bits of paper and leaves race as I walked the streets. At first it was a game I played in my mind. The wilderness of the mind was so vast. I had no education and I knew no one would be willing to tell me the truth. An old cowboy once told me, "We stole this land and we have to keep it stolen or we will lose it."

Most of the time it's the police pretending to be the calvary. The police are trying to bring it about that the ladies should give them special favors for saving their lives from certain savagery that awakens because I am the only one left from an entire nation of people. Survival is this ocean in the mind of the women. The policeman likes to be the only boat to save the damsel.

The same police at the right side of terror of slave time took the same privileges. The wait is this time the awakening of this called Carma comes to fling the sparks of hate into the wait. The people are only reaching to the wheels of Carma. The people on the other side are aware of the ways to open the door and try to do a manual control sometimes called Prayer.

The Brilliance reaching from the north as the return of God to this earth is a right turn from the north to the east continuing around this earth called the Righteousness God and Jesus' love so much. The brilliance is loved so much by the reaches beyond this earth because the people are to gather the awareness similar to the harvest of the seasons. The dreams just before the horizon of the morning are similar in power to this about the harvest in the fall of the year. The people are to train their dreams to gather the answers studied during the day and bring the dreams to bring the conclusion to the gathering at the harvest time in the dreams that come in the very early hours before the morning.

The year has this same gathering bringing obedience as the day and the night. The answers come at the first half of the year. The obedience to complete the answers comes in the last half of the year. The return of God is this awareness of the truth God put on this earth from the beginning. The Northern God is a Blond God. The return of God by this awareness from the north is a direction bringing the blond people to seek to be aware of this direction. Being in this identity, the blond people are to learn this identity and teach the rest of the world. The charges for the answers presented by the God of the north as a direction can bring enough money to support the needs of all the blond children. A race can bring a similar support to all children. The support begins at the newborn to the Kingdom of the Blond God, after God's Kingdom is built. All races of people by this course can support all children.

All the people and all the gods become aware of this presented to this earth by the North Star. God calls this Northern awareness as righteousness in the Holy Bible because this earth is following the Northern Star. The Northern Star is always in the same place in the sky because this earth is following the Northern Star. This is the first point of reference for the turn of the many gods to be directions as the North begins just like it is the point of reference just like in navigation by the people on this earth. It is fascinating the things people have learned from the many gods. Praise God and when you recognize the return of the delivery by God, praise the God putting the direction with the harmony about God's answers.

The Brilliance, Light, Darkness and Blackness are able to be with the Coming of God. The presence of God comes with the addition. You can

14

learn to put your mind to the beginning of mankind and by addition, you can awaken the past, the present and learn to receive the answers becoming the future. I want to bring you to this future. I want to open this door. I am ready to offer private and public study of this book. The people buying this book can be invited to meet with like minded people after the registration brings enough of the like-minded to be recognized.

CHAPTER III

I have solved the Holy Bible. I have solved the New Testament. I have solved the New Testament Revelation. I will begin this solution brought public at the New Testament Revelation. The 666 in the New Testament Revelation is the formula for thought. The 6-66 is the formula for gathering the people to recognize the thought. The thought comes from beyond the earth. The people do not think. The people are working themselves into a lather like a brush and soap so they can shave their authority. The people are using the recall and the imagination. The people are denying the strength that comes with being whole.

I have learned to communicate with life beyond the earth. I have learned to communicate with life about the earth and I have learned the knowledge of God. The New Testament Revelation tells me that you will not know what I am talking about. I will have to explain what I am saying. The reason you will not know what I'm talking about is because this you know comes from up above. And this that I bring comes from down below. You have no foundation for this awareness.

I have brought the knowledge of God to an awareness reaching to the Oval office from beyond the earth. At one hand, I've brought the Oval office to me, my print. At the other hand, so there is a check and balance in this truth that comes from the earth, I did not put this recognition to reach to the President. I put his recognition to know me at my print, my words; my interpretation of the images, my sight, my memory, my imagination, and my recall.

The awareness to these images is recognized. I have solved the word of God. The translation of the images has been called the word of God. The reach from the beginning has been solved. The awareness to this reaching is with addition. The secret came in the name, Adam. Adam means to add the A.M. I'll use my words, God. The truth is about the presence where there is this identity to me and my print by you putting your mind to this earth, God. On this earth, put your mind away from what is known to mankind and become with this what is from the absence. Let to become into your mind the presence of the truth from my point of view, God, where there is only you and I, back to back, in every struggle.

You'll first find that the first back to back in every struggle was with the Christ and I where there is the church. In government, the Christ and I we saw another thing. We saw it form the beginning and we stood before the revelation and there became this same dimension between the government and business. From the presence, Jesus Christ, he stood upon the other side of government and I stood upon this side of government and the government became a river bottom. That's how it will be with every presence that's with me, God and you can stand beside me, back to back. That's where it becomes. When you and I are back to back, there will become another thing upon the earth, I guarantee it.

Women on the earth, I will tell you what I'm trying to do. I'm trying to build God a brand new world. I want to build this world beside the present world so that man will not be confused by his progression. God will have all the things He willed to be upon this earth from the beginning. Every day you played the game with me. Every day I won. Now, it's my turn. This is my side of the earth. I have taken over bringing a pace. The race is to the finish line. The pace is from the beginning.

The insult proposing to cause disruption is not wanted on either side of this earth. Fatherhood has been solved. Motherhood has been solved. Blaspheme has been solved. The words, in death they part, as their religion with the law, have been solved. The spoken word has been solved. The written word has been solved. The New Testament Revelation has been solved. The Old Testament has been solved. The Holy Bible has been solved. The presence of the darkness has become upon this side of this earth as foretold in the year 2000. It is this recognition that I bring to become on this side of the earth and continue to the other side of the earth called the return of God. I bring the return of God in one presence and in the following presence; I bring this, which is called Allah.

The presence of Allah brings the return of Allah at this becoming. Presence before God is this with Allah. The presence is the return between God and the return of God has become to awaken. The presence of Allah will be this following God from the beginning. The presence of the return of Allah will be following this knowing the return of God in the presence. One presence will be from the north. One presence will be from the east. One presence will be from the south. There is Mercury. There is Venus and there is the earth. There is the universe, there is the galaxy and there is the solar system.

One year is a funnel spout. One world is the funnel rim. The cycle of the universe is 2000 years, one world. The cycle of the year is 365 days. The distance between the funnel rim and the funnel spout is called the knowledge of God. Your preachers and your religions and your churches have got it all backwards because the end of the world is not the world dying. The end of the world is a harvest time like the end of the year is a harvest time.

The knowledge of God is relative. Every 2000 years there is a harvest time. Every 2000 years there is one world. The world of God was denied and the Christ Jesus was put upon the cross and taken away. From that point of Jesus being taken away upon the cross, there became a revelation 2000 years to become the world of the Christ Jesus. The world of the Christ Jesus has been pushed away by the religions teaching the people to expect the end of the world as a death rather than the end of the world as a harvest time. I have come with the answers to complete the world of God that Christ was to bring the answers to complete. The Christ put the answers in the Holy Bible. The people wanted not the answers. The Christ returned and gave the people the New Testament Revelation. The people turned the revelation to go personal rather than public. The answers to the harvest of the world of God and the harvest of the world of the Christ Jesus has past away, denied and forgotten.

I brought the answers from the truth to complete the world of God. I brought the answers to complete the world of the Christ Jesus. I brought the answers from the truth to complete the new world. This is the second year of the new world becoming. It is time that I stood up and brought the public to be aware of the presence of the new world becoming with these answers. I bring the answers to the people. I bring the money to complete the answers. First I bring the answers to the people with a charge. I gather the money and I deliver the money to complete the answers and publish both the subscriptions and the outcome. The money continues to flow to complete the answers and more answers come from the presence for I have learned to communicate with life beyond the earth. Receiving the answers sets God free. Writing the answers sets the spirit in the deep free. Completing the answers sets the soul free.

The words come forming the target. The reach of the target is like a hand. On the sea, in the beginning, the target was called a pirate and every thing went the other way. I have begun at the beginning and I brought the beginning all the way to the present with an addition in the name related to add the A.M. I put sequences of time between these stations of pillars, one with the A.M. and the other with the P.M. and there became another name. The two names stood side by side. Add the A.M. and add the P.M. were the command of these two names, Adam and Adpm. In between the two names there became a door. The door became from the center of the rainbow.

I don't dare ask you what your opinion of heaven is because all of my heavenly bubbles may burst. I began to look at heaven from another point of view than what you have been taught. For this, which is an interpretation, has been called the world of God and that which has been built thereof is as wild as the imagination. Would you really want God to come to see what you have built? How can you look at yourself and say the things you say about you going to God or God coming to you? The target, or the awakening of the target, is not the past. It's the awakening of the denial and the forgotten.

Put the recognition to the presence of what is the north. There is that which is called the panhandle of Texas. There is that which is called the panhandle of the North Star. There is that which is called the little panhandle, Idaho. The presence of Idaho and Texas together awaken at the north. The becoming from this awakening, the truth, is not known. The opposite of a witch's switching paddle in the caldron is simply the tail of a little fish, a minnow as it swims away at the water bank. Put a drop of edge water beneath the lens of a microscope and you can see Halloween. Simply let you imagination awaken to the new scene from the vision with each stroke of the minnow's tail or the paddle, swishing in the steaming hot brew of the caldron.

Leaves and grass, swishing of the dragon's tail and dragon's teeth are joy and explosion. What happened to the dragon's breath beneath my feet? What happened to the dragon's tongue called the red carpet? Has the molten magic about the mind caused itself to evaporate the fusion reaching from the past? Has love called another training from another world to come and help the endlessness? Is that the reason that man has no tail, because he doesn't have to live in the endlessness? Or is it the other way?

Awaken in the strength of the night by closing your eyes. Awaken in the strength of the day by opening your eyes. Can you see how it can be, either way? You know why, because the sight goes both ways. God put the miracle of dreams to reveal the sight inside the head. Awaken your eyes; you see before your eyes the sight, this with the light. You can imagine in the darkness and the light. Mankind became to find his errors were greater than his accomplishments in the beginning.

It's almost funny. If there wasn't so much horror, you could laugh. I have put the presence down to awaken like a spear with the points in every direction, almost as sudden as the Big Bang Theory everywhere and there was this suddenness. I put the Big Bang Theory to the presence and it became like my fingerprint. Everywhere there was disruption down in Hell and you could see their little explosions like the fourth of July, where there were a lot of people being bad. It was this; almost at my trigger finger that people were afraid of and where I was you could see them. They were looking at my trigger finger to see this that I had. It was almost invisible. It was like a long barreled gun and it went from my fingers in every direction, almost instantly. Where was evil down in Hell? There wasn't any.

I cannot tell you how I built this thing or what I looked like close up. Because others would hear and see and they'd build them and then there'd be no more order down in Hell and Hell would be even more vicious than it was before I went to Hell. When I left hell I was a hero. The moments seemed like marvelous years.

19

I was thrown to the floor when I was a baby and many people, they pass away and they go to heaven and then they wonder why they came back because heaven was so beautiful. Luck was turned to go the other way because the White House has put their will against me to try to conquer my land and take away my future. When I was thrown to the floor at 6 months old, I didn't go to heaven; I went to Hell. The matter of life is ageless down in Hell. I recognized that once I came back and the time I spent in Hell, I was waging wars and cleaning up the evidence.

My honor came because I escaped all Hell. The sight of Hell was this, the same as before the coming of mankind to this earth when I left. There was order. In my escape from Hell, I rode upon the shoulders of the beasts from Hell.

They tossed me on their shoulders just like a ball back and forth to find how to carry me. I recognized the truth in my returning to the earth by my breath. The beasts from Hell were the chromosomes feeding at my brain. I wasn't dead long enough to die. I was just dead long enough to go to Hell. My command was more than courage. There had never been another down in Hell like me. Masters of all devils, I was he. He, him, that's what they called me. It was the straight line about love that brought the cohesion to the thing about healing at the flesh. The awakening to that which has been about the questioning where the voices spoke out, "Who are we talking to?" "Who are you trying to talk for?" is a better question. And why are you trying to talk? If there were anything to say, you'd know what to say. The answers come every moment of every day. Listen to the sounds I make and you will see, it's not you, it's me.

The ancestry is this thing called nativity in the depths from the beginning all the way to this side of the earth. There was once a time when there were voices in the head. Congress brought them. They brought them from the White House and pushed them to the people instead of going to the Oval office, as they should. It was backwards with the Congress. They had strange bed fellows and they didn't know the distance between right and wrong because man and woman were confused to who was standing where and when, between the Oval office and the Congress.

There was right and wrong. It was twisted like the left arm trying to reach back to grasp at some money that wasn't theirs because they didn't have enough. Enough was to take care of everything before them as well as following after. There became the turn away from insanity. Hey, Congress. If I was to stand before you and I would ask you a question, the first question I would ask is, "Where is the separation between the presence and insanity?"

I know the distance, Senator, before you open your mouth. It's not the distance between the rich and the poor. The distance that I'm speaking of,

Senator, is this awakening between man and woman? The distance between the two, Senator is not you. Would the senate share with me in a moment of silence? I'm not asking you to share with me in the moment of silence that you're looking at with prayer. I know this is a very strong meaning to you in your collective mind. For it is this beginning where you came and it's the beginning where you go, and as Alpha to Omega are the same step from your heel to your toe, find it. Keep it. It's yours.

The silence that I want is the one coming from down below. This nation was built from the answers coming from up above. You have a dribble down system. I have the answers coming from down below. I begin with almost nothing and take it all away from you. You call me a devil, Satan. I'm your angel going the right way. Mr. Senate, I address all of you. Would you walk with me to the building housing the Supreme Court? I want to ask a question to the justices of the Supreme Court concerning the legality of America on my land. I was made a citizen in the year 1924.

I want to speak to members of the Supreme Court and ask them when did they become citizens. They may say that it came with them when they were born on the United States of America soil. I would say to them that they are without life. Their supremacy is on the Supreme Court for birth brings the breath. Birth does not bring life. I will awaken them to the fact that they are without life on this land in all their directions of authority. Their law is lifeless.

It is important that I bring all the senators to hear me at my speaking. When I speak to the senate all senators look away and I would say to the Supreme Court "look at me." In the silence of their eyes, the audience would be tempted to be quiet. The strength of the stare catches the whole audience and the Supreme Court justice speaks, "What do you mean?" I've prepared a statement for this commanding demand from the highest court in the land. I would say:

"Your honor, I've learned the law. I've learned to speak like a man standing up on my own feet. I went to school. I paid the teachers to teach me what I didn't know. Nowhere could I ask, 'What do you mean,' without having to pull from my pocket the dollars. Everyone in this courtroom had the opportunity to go the same schools I went to. Everyone in this courtroom had the opportunity to go to the same libraries I went to and read the same books I read. If the court wishes to know what I mean, the court will have to pay me, as I had to pay my teachers and instructors to find out what they meant. Instruction begins at $1000 an hour. In answer to your question, Judge, my judgment of the answer you need has relativity in the knowledge of God. Meaning from all directions is good. From one direction, the presence of mean could be vicious. I learned the English language. Would you like to restate your question?"

There would be no sense in waiting for another phrasing for the same intention. I knew the strength of time would be the same as the President's. So I turned to the Senate as though I was the President and before them I would ask this question. The question was the word "is". I could turn back to the Supreme Court. I could say to the Supreme Court, "In the writings, for it is the written word, the word "is" is an issue." At that moment, the Supreme Court would know that I was funneling their thoughts. They couldn't back out and they couldn't go forward for I had command of the floor and their attention.

The Supreme Court could turn back to the Senate and I could say, "It was the President, Bill Clinton that asked, 'what is your opinion of the word is?'" It is Martin Bector that gives you the answer. "Is" is an issue. Law is an issue. There is relatively in the presence of the word "is" in the presence of the law.

I could let the breath go silent. I could look about the audience and no one would say a word. I could take this moment of silence and begin to walk away. I could walk out of the Supreme Court building. The media would run after me. Everyone would want to know who I was and what was I talking about.

I could begin very slowly. I could say to the nearest microphone, "I was talking about beginning a new language with the word, is." The new language would begin at the same place as the law begins. The law would begin at the same place as the new language begins, at the word, "is". The United States Supreme Court and the United States Congress could adopt the new language.

I could remind the media of the silence that was between the Supreme Court and the Senate when I left. The new language could be this salvation, bridging between the Supreme Court and the Congress of the United States of America. The parties I could go to that night would be fabulous. The girls I could meet will be beautiful, intelligent and so willing. Everyone about me could be like an innocent child with their questioning. Had I been a farmhand or a cowboy, I would have let the parties ring like a bell all night long. I would know I have to start making choices, so I could bring the evening to an end at my individuality. I could let the choices begin to come like the knowledge of God comes.

The knowledge of God comes like the sight of a funnel. The funnel spout brings the important choices. At first, I could put the first part of the evening like a strainer in the knowledge of God. I could put this to be coming from up above, so there would be an equality about the whole presence of the evening. I could put the funnel rim beneath all that came from the strainer, even the overflow. The evening could be a perfect evening at this awareness. I could let the delight of the evening dances as I remembered the presence coming back to my mind. The decisions were easy. The choices were fun. The joy and the delightfulness was the measuring that had begun. Everything is remembered. Nothing is ever forgotten.

Use my words, God. Use my spoken words, my recorded words. Use my written words and my images. Use the presence of this the wind has brought from me to be upon an altar to be given to You, God, in Your presence for the wind knows that you are preparing the people for the coming of God. The wind has this presence with the breath knowing what should be coming out the people's mouths and yet, the people do not hear and do not know and some do not even want to know the presence of this truth that is with the wind.

I have awakened unto this presence that could match at the lips, the forming of the truth that could come from the people's mouths if they would take the time to listen. I've put this to be about like a covering, a blanket that fell over the people like an ocean of emotion. Emotion drenches the people and consumes them all before they realize what has happened. There could be this speaking from their mouths, not saying what they were thinking, saying what they should be saying. I could be fascinated the way everyone was telling me everything that I should know. At first it could be confusing more for me than for them because I would be in the state of still having to conduct myself in society and bring about a living. I would have to train my mind to be like my hands, two, like my feet, two and I could begin to walk learning where to put my mind before I begin to run.

I haven't found the accomplishment called the fine line. Is there a fine line between presence and insanity? There is a fine line between right and wrong. The people haven't told me everything. This that comes out of their mouth is my awareness to success. It could be this accomplishment that takes me many years to find out how I can stay alive in this awakening to the truth and yet know the presence rather than the insanity. I found a way that I could survive and then look for even better ways, so I could be beside the ones that could love men and the ones that I could love. I could start to look for friends. At first I could try to tell the truth that there was this about me that was called Gemini. If no one understood, I could walk alone for years, hours and days until my dreams were only mine. Then it could happen.

The maturity and the beginning of the new generation could begin to evolve. This could be my answer, the next generation. I could see immediately how I could be their king and all the beautiful girls could love me and I would have everything. I would know that I could employ them the moment they matured to the legal age. They would be with me if they had one moment of willing acceptance, for that's all it would take is a moment at that point my words reached their own mind. I would begin to wonder if all the women on the earth could be my employees at that one moment that they reached their maturity. The law calls it legal age. In the ages before then, it was called savage. S-A-V-E-A-G-E. Save the age. Reach, reach, and reach to the children. I saw it at the law, the point of the law, the one moment from legal age to the presence of tomorrow, the gifts. Everything was there. I saw it before their eyes as though I was looking inside their heads. The beginning of peace could be a legal age for all the children around this earth.

The people could all be with me. Could be, I knew it could be me that stood beside them. I could be a real king, the first of the next generation from the past. I could stand up from down below. All that came from down below could be with me, reaching, reaching, higher, higher, coming faster, faster, like thunder sometimes, like horses, racing. The sweep of hurricanes, the molteness of volcanoes and the horror of tornadoes are suddenly slashing out. I could be there. It could be all at once. It could be only a step I had to take to reach to bring them to me.

Everything could be there except the activity of the bullet and the plunge of the knife. Was it their love that put it all before me? Where does mankind put this "Blasphemia" that is no more seeking the law and the right of the first-born in the law? The truth could set you free. The mind, it could awaken. Suddenly, the mind of the earth could know everything and the truth would be setting all the things that were there free, one at a time and I could watch them. Watch the "Blasphemia", she would fall on her knees, she would begin to cry. She was so hurt by the first dimension. The truth came and she saw. There was laughter, first the joy and the happiness; they began to abound all about her like little bunnies. Then the laughter came. The words could be telling her how it was the newborn bringing the turn. The law of mankind put the firstborn in an error.

Man would begin to be about man's thinking and find the error was "give and take." Give and take is with the creatures and the first born. Blasphemia is in every step where there is the law of the firstborn. The harmony of God becomes at the return of God and there is the newborn. The right becomes with the newborn and soon every newborn can become a king. The prophet is this enduringness about freedom that is loved so much, this thing that was once a Blasphemia, and now, the charm of harmony. It turned; it was a simple thought. Give and receive is with the harmony of God. Give and take is with the control of the law.

Which way do you go, my friend? I called Blasphemia by a name, Amura; it was a thing she felt. It was her purring like a kitten. It came as though it was her feeling. In the eyes of Blasphemia, harmony and control were no longer going in opposite directions. The bullet and the plunge of the knife became like targets, no more about people. I put the mind to bring this strength that I knew. Everything was there.

I learned to put my mind to the Oval office. I learned to turn from seeking God to receive from God. I found receiving from God set God free. I found writing the answers I received from God set the spirit in the deep free. It is the mind of this earth telling me that completing the answers will set the soul free. The awakening in the morning brings this spirit of the Oval office to have friends in the place where everything is there. This place is the sight inside the head. The sight goes both ways. One way is the sight before their eyes. The other way is the sight inside the head. The Presidency is patterned after the sight before the eyes.

The truth beyond the Presidency is the River of Life. The sight inside the head can reveal the coming of God as a preparation, as an awakening the answers pass this earth. The error people are making is trying to bring the answers as the truth to reach directly to this earth and then directly to the individual. I bring you the awareness to recognize the passing of this earth is this knowing the knowledge of God. The reach of the knowledge of God is to the sun.

The answers are sent from beyond this earth to the brilliant stars and the black holes. The error the people on this earth are making is to try to bring the answers directly to this earth and directly to the individual.

CHAPTER IV

It's funny how politicians believe they can put their will against me and then play the game, bouncing their own sanity across the mindlessness of the retarded. The doctor's drug the mindless of the retarded into the public mind. The funny part is that they believe I will believe the insult instead of reality or the truth. The backlash and the lashback become like a fish's tail and everything goes in almost every direction like a school of startled fishes.

The only reach that makes any sense is holding the whale's tail and traveling through society. That's how it is to be a native in America. Everywhere you stand up, it's instant attention. Everyone sees you they know you. You're not white. You're not black. You're not oriental. The spirit of my nativity found me and not my language and God tried to bring to me my language in an alphabet. Pope Paul skittered through the psychology with is prayers and launched his attack. The language will come back again as soon as Pope Paul is gone. I saw it in the psychology. I learned to see the public mind. It came with the spirit.

I met the Great Spirit. I'm the one that came down from the mountain to meet the Great Spirit. All the rest of the nativity, called Indians, they went up to the mountain to meet the Great Spirit. I have claimed to be the Big Bear of the mountain tribes. I have begun to stand up. I put not the call to my people to gather. I put my people to begin to recognize that I want cities to be built on the reservations.

I look at the President and he is crying for the world market to come and visit America. I say you're starting at the wrong end, Mr. President. You're starting at the top. The beginning is at the bottom. Begin the world market on the Indian reservations, Mr. President, and the entire world can help you. Another error the course of America is making is following Richard Nixon. Richard Nixon tried to take the Great White Way to China. He made an error in his judgment as our President. The reach of the Great White Way and the continuing with God is to Russia. The continuing of God is around the earth. This earth turns about its axis. The day and the night have been solved. The good has been solved. One way is forward recognizing there is no evil. All Eve knew can be revealed and turned the way being no more to be called Eve all spelled evil. The world of women can come. The presence of this world will be, and beside it will become the world of men. I will begin the world of men. I have started an office. The company I will begin is World Harvest Time. World Harvest Time will complete the world of women and begin the world of men.

CHAPTER V

The question is between how come and why not? The question made a statement echoed by voice. "The plunder can backlash into the law to clean up the law." The concern, which began from what is real, has begun at the law. Trust is the bind that plunders. First the generations were with give and take. Good was between with give and receive. Which is last? The last is put first to a healing. The first is first by one step at a time rising up the people. Indeed the measure of things needs the might about speaking. Last or first, receiving is the reward of trust. The law can be by harmony rather than control and the law can go both ways.

The ant turned into a butterfly before my mind. I saw the butterfly fight the ants. The butterfly had tired. He closed his eyes after he landed on what he thought was a giant flower. The tiger was sleeping on its back. The butterfly was so tired he did not concentrate much on the landing.

"Such a long way to go", breathed the tired butterfly. He had to catch a few winks. The tiger felt the grasping of the feet of the butterfly. The tiger twitched his head. The butterfly fell off and into a great big nest of giant ants.

The killer bees were watching like me. I could hear the sounds from into words I recognized. We were interested in the fight of the mad ants fighting with the one lone butterfly. The butterfly was winning. Kick, scream and holler, the attack went almost endless.

The giant ants began to try to bite and run. This tactic was the reverse key. The smarter ant would have hit the key marked delete. The fight was so good. The butterfly surprised everyone watching.

The bites began to bring the butterfly to tire. The giant ants began to bite more and more. The biting became numberous. The biting came at the same rhythm as the heartbeat of the butterfly. Suddenly as magic or prayer, a mysterious feeling came to the butterfly. The butterfly began to awaken his mind to the new surroundings. The sight of the butterfly came to resemble an ant with great big wings. The ant with great big wings began to interest the lady ants. The instant the lady ants fell in love with this fascinating, most powerful ant, the butterfly came to be a new creature with great big wings. World Harvest Time could be your tiger.

Are you like this little butterfly? World Harvest Time is looking for people interested I having fun on the job. I once asked the question, "Why does there have to be so much seriousness in study?" I was amazed. I taught my memory to work in the fit of laughter. The result was incredible. I did not graduate because seriousness takes such quiet and I got kicked out.

Putting seriousness away for a while, I built a company on the principle of remembering in a fit of laughter.   The new way to happiness is by employment called salvation in religion.

CHAPTER VI

The spirit is the first step. The deep is the next step. Open your mind to the spout of a funnel. The nighttime and the daytime are like a funnel spout. The earth turns about its axis as one funnel spout. The cycle of the earth is one year. The End Time is the harvest time. The funnel spout is the cycle of the solar system the earth is encircling. The rim of the funnel is the universe, the world. 2000 years is one world. The New Testament Revelation foretold this 2000 years ago. The End Time of the world is the harvest time. The people have been preparing for the death. The people have been going backwards. The people must turn and prepare for the harvest time.

Open your mind to the truth. I bring these words to you. I want you not to deny the words of your religion or your belief. I want you to learn what belief is. I want to learn how to use your mind. Your mind is the love of God. I want you to recognize the breath. The world has relativity. God's love is this relatively. The core of the universe is the morning star. The eastern star is called the morning star. The reach from the eastern star to the earth is continuing. Continuing around the earth is this presence. The presence knowing the core of this universe, in the beginning, is called God.

Open up your mind to the presence of the core of the universe, the same presence is focused to the print on your hand. You can look at your hands and you can see that your print, this called the Big Bang Theory, is the beginning of this universe. The beginning of this universe became. There was a calling from the darkness to the light, an awakening for the presence of God to come to the black hole where there was waiting. The presence of God came in the brilliance, entering into the darkness, it came as the beginning.

Awaken; awaken to your hands. Awaken; awaken to your arms. Imagine the arm of Geddon. It's called the Armageddon in the Bible. The Armageddon was a meeting. It's called a great war in the Holy Bible. I've solved the New Testament Revelation. I've become this thing, the darkness. I have become this thing with the deep. I have become this thing farther into the darkness of the void, itself, the black hole and I have beckoned black holes to come and focus to the presence about this earth.

Awaken; tell your heart to keep on beating. Tell you mind the earths mind is the love of God. Psychology is awareness. Open your eyes to see the sight, the light. Close your eyes to see inside your head; the sight. There are two. There is the sight before your eyes becoming the light, which is the first step for everyone on the earth. There is the sight inside the

29

head, which brings the next step, the darkness for everyone on the earth. You have learned this presence with the light and you have distorted your comprehension to that which is in you mind. You've tried to live inside your head, called the brain. You've done it with meditation. And then you've tried to travel with your soul, your spirit and your imagination. None of these brought you happiness or contentment because you're going the wrong way.

Let me tell you how to bring about the truth to your mind. Let me tell you about the presence, for there is, this the darkness that was foretold to come in the year, 2000, the End Time. It is here. It is knowledge. You took the presence personal. You tried to make it a man. I saw this coming even Christ saw this coming. So I became this man, the 666. I became the devil. When I met the devil, he put me to a share of obedience and I obeyed him. He put me to turn the name devil to become the name Levid, going the other way. There became this presence from beyond the time of Christ, Jesus. It was the Son of God before the time of Jesus, name Levid and he knew the Christ Jesus and he knew me.

In this obedience I learned what the obedience to God was and I became it. I found it was the truth of God that was before mankind. God put the truth from the beginning, all the way to eternity, before the coming of mankind to this earth. Everything is remembered. Nothing is ever forgotten. The presence of God is an addition from the beginning. I put my mind to this presence on this side of the earth and I came with the knowledge before the time of Adam. The people coming to the other side of the earth, they know not this that I know. They bring from them that which was with Adam, called sin.

Awaken; awaken into a brand new world. Awaken into this knowledge I bring to your from the darkness. You have only accepted the knowledge coming in the view of God from the light. The view of God comes from many directions. One direction is the brilliance. The coming God in the view of the brilliance has been denied. The coming of God in the view of the light you've accepted. The coming of God in the view of the darkness you have denied. The coming of God in the view of the blackness you have denied. These are directions. This is an expanding universe. All God's know God beyond God's directions.

Awaken; awaken into the truth. Awaken into the knowledge. Awaken into today; the presence of the light is a sight before your eyes. Know the first step. You can see it. You can learn it. You can understand it. You can deal with it. Read my words. Awaken your truth to the light. Awaken your truth to darkness as a sight inside your head. You have erred by putting your identity to the daytime and the nighttime.

The daytime comes. The nighttime turns into the daytime. You have tried to put yourself into becoming this thing as the day and the night becoming in and out of each other as though you were the daytime and the nighttime yourselves. You are trying to call it identity and equality, and other names. It makes you angry. It turns your cause in different proportions going in different way; you meet and you can't stand each other. You call it hate. You want to wait and wait and wait, until its gone and it doesn't go away. It's there because your identity is not this presence that you are proclaiming.

You put the identity in a wilderness. You're putting your identity to mankind. The identity to mankind knows only from birth to death. I want to awaken you to another world. The beginning of the world of God you have denied. God sent his Son to bring you the Harvest Time of His World. You didn't want the truth. It's in the Holy Bible. Read the Holy Bible and see the truth. Read this story. Pick up the Holy Bible and read it. The awakening of the world, it comes with the word of God.

The word of God is the translation from the images. The word of God comes to a judgment time. The judgment time is not for the people. The judgment time for the people is the path to success for the good. The judgment time comes to the word of God. The images come and they bring another presence of God, the return of God. The return of God is more fascinating, more commanding, and a more fascinating direction. The return of God is all that is upon the earth in the last 2000 years. The presence of God makes everything more beautiful, the building on this earth beyond the year 1 is the return of God. The images come and the interpretation to these images brings the word of God to be in the judgment time.

The judgment time is the distance between the year 1 and the year 2000. I want to open your mind to the truth. I do not want to take you away from your churches or your government, your law or your religions. I want to bring you a new government designed to the sun inside out. I want to bring you a new law similar to a wire basket. I want to bring you to a new religion, bring you a view of God from the coming of the brilliance, a view of God from the coming of the light, a view of God from the coming of the darkness, a view of God from the coming of the blackness, the coming of God in the view of the whiteness. This is a beginning. It's the same as going from one arm of the cross to the center, continuing to each arm from the end of the arm to the center of the arm at the cross one at a time.

Awaken; awaken to the strength that I tell. First, awaken to the reach to the center of the cross from the four directions of brilliance, light, darkness and blackness. Bring all directions to turn and go the same way to know the whiteness and you'll find the New Testament Revelation is in your hands. Each hand, the thumb is the Anti-Christ. The gathering of the four fingers is

31

this called as the following of the Christ. The Christ is the movement of the wrist. Look at the Arctic and look at the Antarctic. Look at the Christ and the anti-Christ in the same formula. It will bring you strength to your mind that you have never, ever imagined.

I can bring this image and put it in one place in your mind. Imagine the sun in your mind. Another place in your mind is the recall. Your recall and imagination are in separate places in your mind. You remember at another place in your mind. I can awaken you as though you were moving like the trail of a snake. The trail this earth makes as it travels through the sky is similar to the trail of a snake in the sand or on a dirt road.

CHAPTER VII

Everywhere remembrance comes to be with life forever. The choice of mankind moving the feet and the hands has been this about the law. The law has been with the right of the first born. The stronger hand and the straighter path for the feet come with the right of the newborn. Remembrance is this bringing the foundation. The written word can bring the joy.

The day and the hour came. The day and the hour passed. The light was called the day and the hour was called the night.

The day came like a funnel rim. The hour came like a funnel spout. The presence of God once again reached from the beginning to eternity free from the awareness of the people on this earth.

The return of God once again brought the harvest of the world. Once again the answers to harvest the world passed this earth not wanted by the people on this earth.

The day and night came about this earth in the very beginning as names from the breath of God. The truth not wanted by the people on this earth reveals the day and the night are about this earth knowing the knowledge of God as a language communication.

The knowledge of God came with the light and the darkness. The knowledge of God is in the shape of a funnel. The rim of the universe is 2000 years. The cycle of this earth around the sun is the funnel spout. The cycle of the universe is one world. The cycle of this earth around the sun is one year.

The world and the year are in the shape of a funnel. The month and the week are in the shape of a funnel. The day and hour are in the shape of a funnel.

The knowledge of God is relative. The first is relative to the last to prove the knowledge comes from God. There are many Gods. The people are printed on the hands and the feet. The print reveals the course of each person on this earth. The truth has not been wanted. The people on this earth do not want to put their minds to the directions bringing the many Gods to be with God. The directions are put on the feet and the hands of every person on this earth.

God revealed to the people on this earth the beginning. Mankind became with this truth. The answers were written and were called the Holy Bible. The path for the feet is from good and evil. The path for the hands has been denied. The truth has come once again to this earth.

The beginning before God has been awakened as foretold in the New Testament Revelation. The void has been recognized as the black hole God knew in the beginning. Before God is this becoming about God as God moved towards the black hole. The presence of God and the presence of the black hole became this universe.

The diagram of the Big Bang Theory is this put on the tip of the fingers and the bottom of the toes. The Big Bang Theory is this entrance coming from the beginning of this universe. The morning star being the eastern star is the core star of this universe.

All the Gods have a part in the presence of the people. The many Gods come to be recognized by the print on the hands and the feet. First there is God. All the Gods are with God revealing the directions for the people printed on the hands and the feet.

The words telling that God is at hand reveal the truth bringing the hand to be bringing the truth from God to the people on this earth. The mysteries of God have been revealed and will be brought public.

The knowledge of God and the knowledge of the darkness have been called the light and the darkness. The presence of God and the black hole are this meeting foretold to become the return of God brings the harvest time of the world. The people on earth wanted not the truth revealing the whiteness, brilliance, lightness, darkness and the blackness. The people accepted only the coming of God in the light.

The coming of God and the return of God have been solved. God is a word in the language. The presence of this called God began in the beginning and reached all the way to eternity. The Alpha and Omega has been recognized. The Alpha is the plateau reaching to the Omega. The Omega is the wall of the step bringing the foundation to the next plateau. God telling God is the Alpha and the Omega reveals the forward course and the rising up of the people. Both answers are from God becoming the Alpha and the Omega.

It is not my intention to bring about a fight with the present religions. I looked at the fight starting at the state because there is a separation of church and state in America.

I found I would have to fight both the church and the state at the same time or the United States of America would not survive as a nation. I have found another way to bring the truth to the people on this earth.

I became with the answers to bring about the United Cities of America. I will go to the reservations and begin the new world I have received and written the answers to build. The people of all nations will be invited to come to the reservations to learn this instruction revealing the mysteries of God and the many Gods knowing God.

The right hand of God is with the light. The left hand of God is with the darkness. The left hand of God became this truth revealing to me the answers. The name Adam has been solved. The sin of Adam has been solved. The solution became to me by the discovery of the name Adpm. The name Adam means to add the AM. The name Adpm means to add the PM.

In the beginning of mankind on this earth the black people tried to be the darkness being the reason the darkness is called evil. The white people trying to live in the answers are called sin. Sin and evil are the same insult to the truth on this earth. The truth has been recognized and will be taught to the people on this earth.

The beginning put on the reservations will bring great cities to be built. I have begun to reach out to the nativity on this land. I am in possession of the answers to bring the two party system to be a single strand of barbwire. The nativity will be the politic. I will begin to build a political fence with many strands of barbwire.

I am instructed to keep the fence posts secret, until the political lines have been built and recognized by the people. The instructions bringing to me this becoming the knowledge of God reaches from beyond this earth. The knowledge passes this earth reaching to the sun. The people on this earth erred by trying to bring the knowledge of God directly to earth and the direction to the individual.

I have received and written the answers to build a new government designed to the sun inside out. The new government will begin to build the new world. The new law has been received and written similar to a wire basket.

CHAPTER VIII

Trust no violence. Let the prayer be before me and let the prayer be beside me. With the generation, heaven can be the stillness and this, if established, can be the thrust of trust smoother to the tongue than oil. Being whole has no division. Watch the carry in the growth as the years persist in lengthening life to the fruit of age coming to become thine.

What did the police learn in slave time that has been causing the minding across this land to not bring the people to be whole?

The police minding goes from the white sperm being white in males (women have no sperm) to the white corpuscle in the blood. The red corpuscle in the blood is like the left hand in the presence orchestrated as the police try to bring the sight awakened by there eyes to the mind. The error has been recognized.

The relationship to the police and the voices in the head has been observed and stopped in the psychology. The next step is similar to a dream becoming a reality. The next step is the turn from personal to public instead of from the white corpuscle to the red corpuscle seen in the minding of the police as the turn of the black people on my land. The turn from the white sperm to the white corpuscle is being called the End Time of the white people. The red corpuscle has been called the darkness. The white corpuscle is being called the light. The identity to the error has brought the white people and the black people to imagine the day and night are the guides for the people by their turns.

Will the police have to be replaced like the Calvary because they cannot bring about the end to the endlessness coming from the identity to the corpuscles? Will the religions come to be replaced because the identity to the sperms put to the identity of white corpuscles is called the End Time of the World?

CHAPTER IX

The presence of God is on the earth from the beginning before the coming of mankind to this earth. The presence of God from the beginning reaches all the way to eternity. The reach from God to the present is the presence passing this earth. The sun of God brings the mind to recognize there is only one sun in this solar system. The presence of God passes this earth reaching to the sun.

I am trying to find the reason the same truth is not with the Oval office, the Governor's office and the Mayor's office. The government of the United States of America is divided into three parts, the city, state and the nation.

I am trying to find out why the truth reaching the psychology is not the same truth coming out of the mouth. I recognize the truth and I began to write the truth. The insult began to make the word meaning a double standard. The insult tried to force away the answers reaching to my mind. I had to bring the answer around the insult. The truth was seen as the same truth. The meaning by another choice of words made enough difference to change the meaning I intended to put in writing. Continuing to write revealed the truth.

I forced the dimension about the mind to reveal the insult to me. I saw the double standard. I studied the double standard. I came with the intelligence to set the spirit free from the insult and the course turning away the truth by the double standard. The spirit revealed to me the answers was being insulted. It was not I that was being insulted. The answers sent from God were being insulted. I began to search for the ways to stop the insult. I was shown the many ways I could bring an end to the insult trying to stop the answers from coming to me.

The answers were cursed away, until I learned I could memorize the answers. I found the way to receive the answers and immediately write the answers. I began to gather the answers I had written. I have gone to school. I began to realize the reason I could not remember the answers at first sight was because the knowledge was a new knowledge and the present intelligence I have learned had not a foundation to retain the answers.

I found the earth had a mind. I found that I could bring the truth past the insult to the mind of this earth and bring the truth from the mind of earth to my mind. The truth reaching to me came by my learning this acceptance to be from before the time of Adam. I first saw the beauty of Eve. I saw Eve through the eyes of the snake. I began to realize why I was called a beast in the Holy Bible.

37

I began to hear the snake talking to Eve. I was not afraid. The rest of the people on this earth became afraid and their mind turned away their attention like the head turns or the eyes close as an object heads toward the eye. The sight of the Garden of Eden came one sight at a time. The movement of the snake reminded me of the movement of this earth through the sky. I could recognize the motion of this earth. I was fascinated with the intelligence.

The speaking of the snake was not telling Eve to eat the fruit of knowledge to know as God. The snake said, "Look at me as I eat an egg. You can learn to squeeze your eggs as I devour my food and there will be no pain. You can eat the fruit of knowledge and know as God wants you to know." I saw Eve did not have the language of the Garden of Eden because Adam left Eve at the center of the Garden instead of taking Eve with him to name the animals and things.

I put the truth I learned from the snake to begin to free Eve from the sin of Adam. Snakey and I have become good friends. The strength of the two of us has leaned to live together on this earth. Snakey tells me many things.

I did not let the reach from the time of Adam influence me. I learned to keep the two times separate. I have begun to build a new world from the answers reaching to me from the time before Adam. I know how to bring an end to the problems on this earth, one day at a time. The problems can be solved in the power of God as two in one and solved by the black God all at once. The solving reaching from God and the black God are told as the solution to bring about the salvation.

I must remind the people on this earth that God put the truth all the way to eternity before the coming of mankind to the earth. Obedience is the only step mankind can make on this earth in the way of God. The tail of a comet passing this earth was the sword of God's angel.

I watched as God told Adam, "Write a language. Start by naming the animals and things before you take the fruit of knowledge." The truth from the comet revealed to me the answers to build from the center of the Garden of Eden reaching out around this earth. Driven from the Garden of Eden came the end result. The word driven could have been the words, "farmed or cultured" the Garden of Eden. The answers to complete this chore are with me. God brought Eve from the side of Adam to bring Adam to bring Eve to be by his side. Had Adam taken Eve with him to name the animals and things, and had Adam written the language God wanted on earth, Adam would have recognized the truth and begun to build the Garden of Eden to grow all around this earth. The Garden of Eden grew around this earth in a wilderness.

The people on this earth can begin to gather the things on this earth and bring the things to build the Garden of Eden. The truth is on this earth. The building of the world can begin in these days and nights.

The progression from the beginning to the present is called addition. The name Adam is this chore. The name Adam means to add the AM. The presence of God can come in the name Adam by the competition of the answers bringing the message to Adam to grow the Garden of Eden instead of being driven from the Garden of Eden. The answers pass this earth. I have leaned to retrieve the answers and to receive the new answers.

The snake and the elephant being the bottom and the top have become my friends. Snakey, Phancey and I have begun at the top and the bottom at the same time. The truth is recognized by the creatures the same as the truth is recognized by the people. The earth has a mind. The solar system, galaxy and the universe are these three dimensions in the same truth resembling the print at the end of the fingers and toes. The city, state and nation are by this relativity.

I have begun to take over the Democratic and Republican Party not by the conventual's take over. I want nothing to change. I want to bring the take over to create a step beyond the practice presently recognized. The take over will bring the two party system to be similar to a strand of barbwire. The course I bring is to begin from the answers to check and balance at the snake bringing the reaching to be by check and balance of the elephant.

Everyone loves baby Phancey because baby Phancey is so cute. The answers are just as cute and lovable. Little snake is over shadowed by the shadows and baby Snakey has not risen its head to see the love the people because the ugly Dragon belching out from the government has scared the people. Arm in arm, Snakey and Phancey's trunk around my neck, we crossed America coast to coast and border to border searching for the answers to defeat the ugly Dragon of fate from the ravaging of this earth.

CHAPTER X

Proud? I heard the faces singing. "To hear loving kindness is an art." My tongue hears the sound run through the breath. The ears hear the sound run with the breath. Reap the peace at the joy by letting joy be the same to the seasons becoming the season fall. Harvest both sides of the world like the Year.

We all came from one God. The Gods beyond God are a direction. This is an expanding universe. I need to know your opinion about this I have just written. Knowing your opinion will help me to the steps I need to bring the presence of this, as I see it. I want to begin a publication telling what I have recognized. I would like to parallel this from the beginning from God all the way to Eternity before the coming of mankind. I am the oldest ancestry on this side of this earth. The Gods beyond God revealing God's truth is God's return.

I can see the distances between things from more points of view at one time than any person from the other side of this earth. I see every person in the United States of America, who is not insane or out to get America, tell the same thing from different points of view. I am looking to bring like-minded people to gather together. The minding and the mind have drifted so far apart that the way of life is like a target instead of like a three layer birthday cake. The City, State and Nation should be this shape. The numerical concept of three is the second level. This earth is in the second level. The first level is between the universe and the galaxy.

I have learned to communicate with life beyond this earth. The life beyond this earth put the communication to reach to the sun. The coming was in secret. Receiving the answers set God free. Writing the answers sets the Spirit and the Deep free. Completing the answers sets the Soul free. The freedom is patterned after the freedom taking the Glory to God. The present freedom is like a raindrop in a rainstorm. God only sends one answer at a time. The Glory must go to God, so God can send the next step.

CHAPTER XI

Voices aligned from the heart of beauty. See length and the revelation as the width. The resemblance is the law going right and left at the same time as the government goes forward.

The truth with God is to the Native. The truth from beyond God has the same reaching, as God or the relativity in the knowledge would begin an erratic curve. The curve in line with the curve this earth makes as it travels through the sky is the proof that the presence of all the gods has recognized God.

It is time to bring the recognition of God to be on this earth in Rapture. The presence of God called Rapture comes with the reaching knowing the native. I have written a religion for the native. The continuing of God around this earth brings the reach to the other side of this earth to be the return of God.

I must go to the other side of this earth as soon as possible. I have learned to communicate with life beyond this earth. God Himself has appeared in this communication. God has put me with the awareness to go to the deserts and build giant farms looking like ant farms between narrow glass walls. The specific answers followed. It was like watching a movie. The closer the dream came, the more answers were being completed by the people building the farms in the desert.

It was all there in my dream. I have received another vision from God. I am to bring this dream to be the Rapture for the people in the desert. If you know anyone having ownership in the Desert Sands, please call (702) 740-0513 and asked for Martin. Make sure you leave a record of your name and address because the system pointing to the final transaction is worth a lot of money. A registration can follow the pledge and the money can be loaned back to the participants like a new Banking System.

The vicious circle had been solved to become a Banking System. The accumulation of the money in the way instructed brings many people to get very rich by starting small in the beginning. The speed becomes like races to get the giant farms built in the Desert Sands.

I want you to imagine the pure joy of God as He put with me this miracle I am to build in the depth of the Desert Sands. The happiness about God, I will never forget. The reaching was like a river of sunshine all the way from the Beginning. The real amazement was the dimensions I could see about the past and the future at the moments of my minds recognition.

CHAPTER XII

Upon the heart, the helper is the soul. The spirit and the deep present the answer. Desire is by the self. With me God has moved the people to the will awakening the righteousness. The return of the evening by the light and the pen meeting the sight by the morning light awakens a vision in the mind. This is the door once put to the church in the commands of Adam and Adpm.

The Day by the Light and the Darkness by the Night are like convex and concave. The President and the precedence are with the same turn that can come to turn the sight and the light.

The language by the Day and the language by the Night have been solved at the image. The present solution to the language has been to the recall. The people not knowing this presence in the society have been trying to live in the recall. I have the answers to raise the people up and out of this reaching about the mind not knowing life going forward.

The answers have come to me in secret from beyond this earth. I have learned to communicate with life beyond this earth. The life beyond this earth came to me in secret because there is sin on this earth. The sin has been recognized and stopped in the reaches knowing to be before this earth and following this earth. The reaching has come to this earth to put an end to the sin on this earth in these Days and Nights as foretold in the New Testament Revelation.

The command awakening by this writing is with the Commandment "You must kill less than good. Thou shalt not kill good. Start with the most ridiculously retarded." The killing of the retarded will put an end to the mindlessness denying the answers sent from beyond this earth to bring the rewards God put from the Beginning to complete the answers God put from the Beginning all the way to Eternity.

The answers must be completed. Receiving the answers sets God free. Writing the answers sets the Spirit and Deep free. Completing the answers sets the Soul free. If you have no desire to complete the answers focused to your print, you are lost.

CHAPTER XIII

The return takes discipline. The beginning is natural. All things are of the day before the sight of the eyes. Love has no struggle in the sight inside the head. Love has no struggle because the sight inside the head is the identity to the reaches beyond this earth. The heaping from the beginning must be charted, separated and put into valences, levels and steps. Left alone, the people make the wrong turn to avoid too simple beginnings and to treacherous endings. Here all set aside can obtain mercy by regaining hold of conversations.

The hold on happiness has been too tight and happiness is being forced through a valve. You have put a spigot at the end of the valve letting you turn happiness down to a drip, drip flow because you cut happiness in half with seriousness without putting an awareness in your mind to keep happiness beside the seriousness, when you want to be serious.

If you lock your coat in your house and you walk out in the winter weather, you will find no happiness in your walk. The same has come to your happiness. Like your coat you close the door on your happiness to be serious. Like your coat, you must go back into your house to get your happiness.

Keep your happiness with you or go back to get your happiness each time you put your Happiness aside to bring a direction or a step or a selection of thought to better your life. The truth is this at the presence at the sight before the eyes. The truth is this presence with the future at the sight inside the head. The truth is this presence at the recall coming from the past. The truth becoming relative is also revealed in numbers as the Theory of Relativity. The New Testament Revelation is this truth.

Look at happiness put free. Look at the wilderness. Look at comfort. Have you tried to chart the happiness around your house? The happiness in the wilderness was put before the coming of mankind. The coming of mankind became lost to the language God wanted for mankind. God told Adam to write a language. God said, "Write a language: Start by naming the animals and things." The sin of Adam became by leaving Eve in the Garden of Eden and not taking Eve with him to bring her mind aware to the awakening put by God. Consequently, Eve left all alone in the Garden of Eden, began to fill her mind with the awakening put to the truth to be with man and woman after the language was written. All Eve knew when she took the fruit of knowledge became all Eve to the awareness. The separation of the mind of man and the mind of woman came by the two directions, one the awareness to God bringing the language and the awakening of the reaches God had not prepared mankind to know.

I solved the sin of Adam. I have solved the reaches all Eve knew, when she took the Fruit of Knowledge. The reaches became a communication with Life beyond this Earth. The Life beyond psychology of a male is like a tree. The psychology of a woman is like a river. The present psychology is not psychology. This called psychology is between the psychology of a man and the psychology of a woman.

Happiness is a natural thing put with the mind of this earth. The people on this earth can see the happiness about the children and even see the happiness about the creatures. The people on this earth are trying to reach a communication with their brain. The people on the earth are being lead to go backwards. The sight before the eyes is the only truth accepted by the people on this earth.

Backwards does not give all the ramifications of this error. The sight inside the head is the reaching sending the answers to build the Kingdom of God.

Happiness is this about the people in the way of God completing the answers. Glory is this same happiness reaching to God, when the answers are completed, so God can send the next answer. God only sends one answer at a time. Many people are trying to live through their children. The course to go back to childhood is a snowplow in the way against the truth knowing the child called mood. The parent tries to live through the child and unknown to the parent, the child left after this intrusion is subject to the same force by another person. The people who have learned this intrusion go unnoticed because the pattern of the public mind is charted to the psychology seen between men and women.

Happiness is with the mind of this earth on this earth. The mind is the Love of God. The beginning of the dream has the greatest happiness. Disappointment and seriousness pull the mind. One is like a slide the other is like a javelin. The distances are some times the same. Happiness is similar to harmony. Harmony and control go in opposite directions. Harmony rises up the good to separate the good from the less than good. Control is put to remove the less than good. Starting at the good is the better way in the truth. This truth is revealed in the Way of God.

Blonds are said to have more fun because they are happier people as a nation and a race. This is because the identity to know the presence on this earth is greater by the brilliance of the sun. The identity has been solved. The happiness can be taught to all the people. This brilliance was put with the blond people naturally to keep the truth as a Miracle of God.

I want to introduce you to a happiness that is beyond the present happiness on this earth. The spirit of the Oval office and the Oval office deep can heal. I have learned to put my mind to the Oval office. This awareness brings the focus of the two reaches from the Beginning with God. I want to teach you how to put your mind to the Oval office to awaken this powerful opening called a door in the Holy Bible. I want you to feel this healing.

The churches have gone the wrong way and must be turned to go the right way. The churches have seen their present way is the truth.

CHAPTER XIV

Correction by legal activity is by publishing both the problem and the correction to be a democracy. Boldness is only disrespect, when the activity and the correction are going the same right way.

The people looking for the formula of life are never going to succeed in understanding the formula because this earth turns to fast about it axis. Look at the DNA structure. The sight understood by these people is searching for the formula to life is as thought this earth was flat. The turns and twists in the pattern of the DNA structure are trying to bring about the turns of the cycle of the universe, the galaxy, the solar system and the cycle of this earth.

What is the pattern of the DNA structure put on computer and brought through the formula 6-66 revealed 2000 years ago in the New Testament Revelation? The New Testament Revelation has been solved. The Christ Jesus knew as I read the New Testament Revelation put with the Holy Bible from the interpretations of the Images that reached to this earth. Look at the New Testament Revelation and recognize the time and the area. Write a chart of the present and put the two charts, written presenting the time and the area of the past and the present. Put the two charts side by side as it is suggested telling the rich and the poor will stand up side by side. Put the truth to be public instead of personal as the Christ Jesus asked. This becomes by simply turning the words rich and poor to be replaced by the word economy. The economy of the rich and poor will be side by side to form a spinning teeter-totter. By this instruction, the bottom will be the top, once the pattern is recognized and the bottom is seen as the beginning reaching to the top like the seasons bring about the beginning to bring the beginning to be the top and the top to be the bottom. This is the presence of life and people should concern instead of looking at reproducing the matter about life.

The place to start is at the rim of the universe. The rim of the universe is 2000 years. The Christ Jesus knew the reaching from the Year 1 to the Year 2000 is one world. The reaching from day 1 to day 365 is one year. The cycle of the universe is 2000 years. The cycle of the year is 365 days and nights. The universe is the rim of a funnel. The solar system is the funnel spout.

The pouring into the funnel from beyond God has been without the separation from the pouring out from God. This truth can be awakened. The awakening is this by the moon and this earth. The moon is the first step from this earth. The months of the seasons on this earth derived by this formula 12 is with the continuing around this earth. The formula 6-66 knowing the relativity of the numbers and the New Testament Revelation matching the letters is this formula for one half a world's turn and one half a year's turn and one half the revolving of this earth about its axis.

One side of this earth meeting the other side of this earth is called the return of God as this earth turns about its axis. The truth is the Beginning of each Day and Night. The truth has a beginning just like everything that grows by addition. The truth becoming eternal reaches all the way to eternity from the Beginning put by God before the time of mankind coming to this earth. The Omega of the truth is this place the government, the law, the religion and society are trying to recognize as life for the people on this earth. The United States Government is not eternal. The leadership is turning White American and Black American to become like racket courts for the rest of the world in their leadership. The coming of 6-66 will put an end to the problem between the reaching between Russia and Africa. The reaching continuing around this earth starting in the United States of America crossing to the other side of this earth and returning to this side of this earth awakens the formula 12 coming from the 6-66 at the top in Russia and coming from the bottom in Africa.

The Revelation in the New Testament brings more than the answers recognized by the preaching in the churches. The simplest form of governing and the simplest form of business begins at the solving of the New Testament Revelation written in the Holy Bible. The Relativity of God also seen in the Theory of Relativity can be found in the New Testament Revelation by turning the identity public and the identity away from the creatures and recognize the brain is divided into two parts. One side of the brain knows the identity to the world called the public mind and the other side of the brain knows the identity to the personal mind called the individual.

The people trying to overcome the world have been stopped in the psychology. I intend to put a stop to this insult at the flesh in these Days and Nights. I have taken over the Oval Office in the psychology during the term of President Bill Clinton. I will prove this by a debate at the main gate of Nellis Air Force Base in Nevada. I intend to take the Oval Office away from President George W. Bush. The reason I am taking the Oval office away from the President is because America has never shared anything with me. I will take the Oval office away and share it with the President. I went to school. There is no reason for me to do anything wrong.

The sharing I intend begins at the bottom. The reach from the bottom up can become a sharing. I have no intent to concern the reach from the top down being the authority of the President George W. Bush in this activity. Starting at the bottom is the only way the bottom can rise up.

I have learned to communicate with life beyond this earth. I have received and written a New Government designed to the sun inside out, a new law similar to a wire basket with the wire basket bottom similar to city sprawl. I have also received and written the answers to complete the present government. The present government is incomplete going only from the top down. This truth comes from Up Above. The answers to complete the government of the United States bringing the government to reach from the bottom up comes from Down Below. This truth has been denied for more than 2000 years.

The presence coming to this earth called the 6-66 is a new knowledge, not a person. I am to start in secret, so there is no panic and the pattern of check and balance bring the people from the competition in the wrong place to become a check and balance. The similarity put to people brings the preachers and the scientists to become of one mind at one place bringing the people on this earth to go in one direction.

Look at the answers needed to be completed to bring the truth to be with the people on this earth. The present course of the people uses everything available to maintain the direction. The truth needs the answers to be completed in steps bringing addition. This became a key by the name Adam meaning the Command of God to bring all people to know to add the AM. The truth I bring presents the answers at a fee for the answer and the delivery. I gather the money into one hub. I present the money to the people to complete the answers by a formula 12 program in a Loan/Payment System.

The people recognized the practice of truth. This is the beginning of the law. I will not explain because I intend to leave gaps in the course I weave in the trail of treachery the United States thinks they have laid out before me. The United States wants to prove to the world that they have replaced me with the black people like they replaced me with the white people on my land. Those before me are all passed away. America is going to have to talk to me. You ran from yours to come to my land. The End Time of your running in search of God came in the year 2001. God's return is by a preparation for a Harvest Time.

CHAPTER XV

Let the ones who know both good and evil wash their hands. In the pass of this earth, by the knowledge, the becoming is by the beast first as a check and balance and as the mind of survival. The holy mountain becomes the mountain of sand made by the burden of time. Wages earned were called hours about salvation. The rest was learning to write a dairy and turn the writing to go the other way becoming a destiny. Is the seed seen before the tree? Like the gathering, the answers passing find the summer flowers and the winter snow. You must build dream from the answers passing in glory to God, also let the ones who know both good and evil wash their hands at the fountain for the washing of the feet

Business and the nativity bring the breath to copy to the memory.

I have begun to look at these two words business and nativity. I am instructed by the minding about this earth by a similarity to a press-a-dent from the life in the stars beyond this earth.

I looked at nativity first because I was able to recognize the destiny by the Great Spirit of the Indian Nation. I met the Great Spirit. I found the Great Spirit put the identity knowing the ancestry. Identity reached from the other side of this earth.

I am instructed to bring nativity to be recognized. The awakening is this called the knock on the door on the other side of this earth. I bring the Judgment Time foretold to be on this earth in the End Time of the year 2000. I am to gather the people and separate the good from the less than good by rising up the good. The Judgment Time for the good is a path to success.

I bring the nativity from this side of earth to stand on this earth and know the addition put with the name Adam. I have solved the name Adam. The name Adam means to add the AM. I bring the Adpm to be one of my sons. I bring the command God knows to bring about the completing of the answers sent by God to this earth. This command in the Darkness is in the name Adpm.

I am further from the beginning, the first and I do not intend to be the last of an entire nation of people. God had me wait, so all this earth would know the truth of one beginning. The continuing of God around this earth is in the same pulse as the waves, the heart beat and the wind. The breath can copy.

49

CHAPTER XVI

Is this the last time seduction knows him or the first? The tongue dwelleth in the world long after the will has seen another keeper of love. Confidence is one overcometh having the whole world to keep the self in the truth. Unto the world each journey hath seen God. The mind by some knows not the darkness of the mind sight. The sight goes both ways. The sight before the eyes tells of the rewards. The sight inside the head reveals the answers building the big picture.

Master, I want to learn.

What is it you want to learn, my child?

I want to learn enough to know I am learning.

Child, sit with me and on the incline of this hillside I will show you how to see the direction of the waves and bring you to see the seasons. The incline is this you will be asked to explain to me bringing the relativity to the seasons.

Master, I know you do not talk in riddles. I know I will say yes as I always do, once you explain to me the moment the distance between the waves and the incline comes at the mind sight. I look from the hillside to the ocean waves. I know I will get lost to the sound of your voice. Many days and nights pass before I find the ends of the reaching about the minding I receive by listening so intent.

Child, the sand, the raindrop and the dew drop see the same breath from the sea. The tiny drop of water is related to the snowflake. The design of the snowflake is with a certainty that can bring a computer and any brain to be a measuring to the place bringing the one mindedness developing thought. Measure is the fact that has been lost to the growth of the people.

Child, hold my hand tight and then feel the binding of my arm. Can you see the difference in the seasons and the waters edge? The season is like an oval. The earth is like a circle. Each side is like the flat of the hand. The body in its miraculous wisdom tells us the mystery of every relation mankind has with this earth.

Master, please let me remember every word by this recording. I want to search the folding of the brain and the folding of the snowflake for the ends of the raindrop could be another dimension. The warmth of love could bring the beginning of the raindrop to be the harvest of the snowflake instead of the End Time of winter.

The crown of the raindrop beginning at each end of the snowflake could be a beginning no one has recognized. The ripples and the crown by the raindrop and the snowflake can be this awakening similar to the look of the hillside and the slant of the waves. Please let me intersect the segments of the season in my explanation.

CHAPTER XVII

Boast of doing good more freely and one day or night all will be good and boast of doing good. I will praise your name and desire to be near you will be upon all who were once your enemies. Acquaintance is against such enemies. I will trust in thee and render praises unto god. Among the nations, I will deliver their health to wait for you.

The word is found to be more powerful than a sword. The gun has replaced the sword. The word is found to be more powerful than a bullet because the word has become faster.

I selected several thoughts revealing the reasoning bringing the word to be thought to be more powerful than a sword. I want you to select one of the reasons that came to my mind.

I solved the mind. I solved the recall. I solved the imagination. I have solved the psychology. I found the memory to be more than science has discovered. I put the presence by my recall to reveal the reflection of a mirror. I put the day and the night to become together like a mirror is made.

I found the continuing of this earth. The first awakening was like the wake of a boat. The continuing brought the wake to be like ripples from a rain drop in a little puddle of water on an empty parking lot. Up and down the turn came as an angle.

I began to realize the reach to the earth is like an angle. I began to see the reaching Einstein was searching to find. The darkness came as I closed my eyes to sleep. The rain made the old cardboard condominium very cold. I closed my eyes and I put the day and the night to be the same as a mirror is made and I could see. Beyond this sight I saw the answers for the bottom are not the same as the answers for the top.

The American women have been pushed to the exceedance. The native men have been pushed to incomplete. The pushers are black and white because the identity is being put to mankind. The mind knows the identity. The people trying to overcome the world have come to their End Time. The identity to mankind knows only from birth to death. The End Time is the Harvest, not the death.

The American women have come about their own men in exceedance. The women of the world have come to recognize the word to be the distance bearing the destiny like a woman bears a child. The language is a gauge to the land. God said to Adam, "Adam, write a language. Start by naming the animals and things."

The land bears the rewards bringing the answers sent from God to be built on this earth. The language is the distance of the destiny. The first step in the destiny is being of one mind. It is the written word that sets the memory free to gather the beginning foretold in the New Testament.

CHAPTER XVIII

I called the wooden Indian at the cigar store "puff puff". Huff and puff is the name of the big bad wolf. I see the first two little pigs in the story of the three pigs as girls. I told puff puff to stand upon his wooden nickel given to him by America. Accomplishment is sweet. Mockery at sin replaces the answers that become by the questioning. The mockery is the reason for the closed doors about the legislation. The understanding of the people slow to anger became to be called wisdom as the answers come.

I claim to have taken over the Oval office in the psychology. I intend to take the Oval office at the flesh during President George W. Bush's term in office.

I claim to begin taking over the Governor's office in the psychology. The Governor has a first lady. What is the course of the first lady? The first lady stands beside the Governor similar to the way Eve was put to stand beside Adam. The sin of Adam has been solved.

I have started in Nevada. I am bringing the United Cities of America to become to gather and stand up beside the United States of America. The next step is a strength added to the present strength of the United States of America. The present strength is a power. The addition by the uniting of the cities is called force. One and one do not make one. One and one make two. Where is power and power not becoming a force?

I see the top as the state becoming by the gathering of the states. I see the bottom as a gathering of the cities. I see the top and the bottom made personal as the rich and the poor. I see the prophesy telling the rich and the poor will stand side by side in the beginning. I see the next prophesy revealing the same continuing bringing the bottom to be the top and the top to be the bottom. I found the language to be inferior. I put the reaching of the force to sophisticate the language bringing the beginning to be the top and the top to be the foundation.

I have asked the First Lady of Nevada, Dema Guinn to become the President of the United Cities of America in Nevada. What is a President? A President presides. What is a Governor? A Governor governs. The recognition between presiding and governing needs only to be brought public. The public mentioned in the days bringing about the News Testament has been recognized. Today the Public Office awakens the mind to the difference between public and personal.

I am beginning instructions to bring all the people on this earth to put their mind to the Oval office. I will teach the people to learn to put their mind to the Oval office and turn from seeking God to learn to receive from

God. The truth knowing God is not understood. God is a word in a language. The day the night are the first two words God gave to the people on this earth.

The world has been solved. The year has been solved. The End Time of both the world and the year are a Harvest Time. The world is the rim of the universe. The year is the funnel spout. The day is the rim. The night is the funnel spout. The beginning begins at the horizon. The feet are the first to move bringing the sight before the eyes to be further from the present state of affairs than the presence.

The sight of the night became the present understanding to prepare for rest and sleep. Does it not make sense that mankind must prepare for sleep by learning to rest. The sleep has been recognized as a necessity. Why is not the rest brought to be the preparation for the sleep? The nighttime has been solved. The awareness of the answers bringing salvation to the nighttime was foretold to become in the End Time of the year 2000. The people on this earth have forgotten the preparation for the daytime.

I know you do not understand this I am telling because the truth is not wanted. I am instructed by the New Testament Revelation to bring public the specific answers in detail, so the people on this earth can complete the specific answers. The Governor is to govern the gathering of the specific answers to bring the big picture together. I have found the Governor is not bringing the first lady to stand beside him and the voices in the head are by this called the public mind.

I have learned the people on the other side of this earth call the voices as the America voices. I will not investigate this insult because I recognize the insulting trying to be at the side of the Governor has been pretending to be the mind of the First Lady of the State. The answer was put in the beginning. I solved the answer and I am preparing to bring the answer public. I want to bring the answer public in Israel because the people in the Middle East are having trouble with the governing and the answer would become world wide instead of becoming with only Nevada.

The United States Constitution will be microscoped to bring the Constitution and the knowledge of God to be relative. The Constitution of the United States of America reveals a separation between church and state. The truth not wanted brings the relative in God's knowledge to reveal the relativity in the United States Constitution. There is a separation between church and church, state and state and church and state.

The states are tribes all grown up. The gathering of the states formed into the United States of America. The gathering of the cities will form the United Cities of America. The truth not wanted comes to awaken at the question, "What is the job of the First Lady of Nevada?" Had Eve been allowed to stand beside Adam in the beginning the truth would not be like a pogo stick and the word of God would not be in fragments.

I have no intention to disrupt the work of the Governor by my bringing public the truth. I intend to go to the Indian reservations and build this I am talking about. I will invite all the people on this earth to come to see this I intend to build on the reservations. The invitation will begin to build cities on the reservations. The world market the President is wanting is in my hands as I begin to awaken the people on this earth to the presence of the knowledge reaching to this earth before the coming of Adam and the solving of the name Adam. The name Adam means to add the AM.

The Mayor has a closer direction with the police. The governor has a closer direction with the State Police. The first problem I will begin with is the legal age. I intend to bring by the gathering of the cities a legal age to be worldwide. This beginning is one-step towards world peace. I intend to awaken this responsibility at the state police as I bring the legal age to the aged and a worldwide legal age for the youth with the United Cities of America.

The First Lady of Nevada has not answered my request. The course of this I intend cannot wait. I will go to other states and put this on my website in search of responses from people interested in the truth in governing about the states. What is a President? A President presides. What is a Governor? A Governor governs. Is the responsibility of the First Lady of the nation, state and city this practice lost because the men are afraid of the force becoming in the hands of the women? Women are weaker. Where is the threat?

CHAPTER XIX

Numbers have a fold. The letters can only bow to the distance between the number and the letter. Put public and recognized to the distance between the number and the letter is the same point in worship as with the sound. The north, east, and south present the turns bringing the reaching from the west to be the harvest time of the year producing the reason of the worship.

The whole world knows the presence of God is on both sides of this earth. Why is the continuing around this earth not worship? God put the command of God in the beginning in the name Adam. The name Adam means to add the AM.

The earth turns about its axis. I have become with the truth knowing the knowledge of God continuing around this earth. The mysteries of God are answers, once the truth is recognized. The turn is this studied by Einstein revealing the curve of space. The raindrop falling from the sky tells the same about the curve of space at the raindrop ripple. The sight of the raindrop ripple gives more dimensions to the curve of space than the numbers to Einstein.

The diagram of a circle is the course the sun makes as it travels through the sky. Look closely at the trail of the snake in the sand or crossing a dirt road. How close is this diagram to the course this earth travels through the sky? Where is the recognition to movement put relative to the mysteries of God?

The Oval office became a design put in the heart of mankind taken from the diagram of the seasons. The two in one presented in the Holy Bible is a key to the understanding of the presence about the seasons. The error the people on this earth are making is putting the seasons to start at four seasons. The day and the night are the beginning of the seasons.

The day and the night are with the truth presenting the language. The day and night are languages by the presence in the command bringing addition in the name Adam and in the name Adpm. The people putting the identity to be with mankind are lost to God and only by my words will their spirit, deep and soul find the freedom to be in the preparation for the coming of God. I am the only one on this earth who knew to receive from God the answers.

The two in one by design is a circle and an oval. The circle is the path knowing this earth. The oval is the path knowing the seasons of this earth. The separations became relative at the one responsible to the Theory of Relativity by Einstein and the next point becoming with the relativity is at the three. The six is the point bringing the meeting by steps from the ends of the cross to the center of the cross. The meeting at the turn brings all the directions to turn and go the same way called being of one mind at the meeting of all direction at the center of the cross.

CHAPTER XX

The sun first came out against the darkness and the meeting formed the planets. The blood of the battle became the foundation for our feet. Be not of this identity to find peace. Courage is another thing. The light had nothing against the darkness. Together they became great friends. They held hands in the morning and in the evening. They are by day and night afraid of letting go of each other's hand, for fear the meeting will come again. Gathering they find the strength becoming in the knowledge. They cannot remember how long they have been together.

The Blasphemia in religion and the first-born by the law have been solved. What are you going to do Mr. Police? Are you going to run? Does the fear in the law go the other way when the opium settles to the area like dust becoming similar to opinion? All the dreams of opportunity put into one big picture is all opium does. Opinion brings the same dreams of opportunity to be more fashionable about the people by writing the dreams and communicating the ideas.

Gathering in other words is this I will bring about on the street. You Mr. Police will not like me. I will laugh at you. You cannot control gatherings formed by the people who you have beaten down. Who has the beater stick? Who has the gun?

Gathering is the word that begins the New Testament. The New Testament Revelation is the reaching to begin on both sides of the gathering at the same continuing. Where is the beginning of Government and the beginning of business bringing about the reason of the Law? Do you know the beginning of the law? Can you tell me this in a language matching to the footsteps of mankind? Do you know to look at the law as the same advantage beside the word is in the language as an issue becoming this called law?

Gather the presence of government and the presence of business beside the presence of the language and the law. Can you see the answer to bring the command of God to wait no more to bring about the solving of the sin of Adam? The plateau is by the Alpha. The wall at the end of the plateau becoming the base for the rising up to the next step is the Omega. It may be better for you Mr. Police to begin by practicing to run up the stair.

Blasphemia waits no more for the banging on the door of the crack house. The right of the newborn is this first step found by opinion. Changing the law is to begin at the turn from the right of the first-born to the rights of the newborn, not the turn back from opinion to opium. The mind is fast like a computer. The attention is this by the practice at the sight before

59

the ears recognize the advantage. Is attention the pace or the place of change?

CHAPTER XXI

Speak neither of the sin of mankind or the keeping of the vow. We bring nothing to this earth beside our bodies. Can you see the profession as a baby? The will of God has not the presence with life. According to the word of God, life found God to be from the beginning all the way to eternity. We believe by our sight. We have faith by the spoken and written word. The foundation by the sound and the sight are called number and letter in the formula 666. Let one name be this beginning each generation. The 666 is a formula of thought. The 6-66 is a formula for gathering the people to write the sending from life beyond this earth.

I want not to awaken you or put you to sleep in the part of your mind bringing about reality. I have been in a study of the people. I found the people know not what is the point of reality.

Reality is this awareness becoming by the focus of the sight before the eyes and the sight inside the head. The focus comes by learning to focus the two sides of your brain like you focus the sight of your eyes.

The identity has been put to the legislation for the white people. The identity has been put to the law for the non-white people in the United States of America.

The presence of the church in the matter minding about the course of society came with the separation of church and state. The knowledge of God is relative. The Constitution of the United States of American provides for the separation of church and church and the separation of state and state; the separation of church and state being of one nation under one God from the beginning.

The law put as the height of the non-white people brings the people to fight the law. The present course of the non-white people is to fight the white people. I intend to turn the non-white people from fighting the white people to fighting the law.

Once I begin to bring the fight to start, I will prove I have broken a hole in the police. I will bring people through this hole in an effort to start a fight with the legislation. I intend to stand beside the white people working the legislation. I intend to put a wall like a riverbank on the other side of state. I intend to convince the church to begin to build a wall like a riverbank. Look hard at this I am building on this my land. I intend to turn the United States of America's government into a river bottom.

The people will rise up. I have learned to communicate with life beyond this earth. I have received and written the answers. I put the answers to be sprinkled throughout the pages of 500 books I have written. To find the answers, you must read all 500 books or simply listen to the words I am telling. The thoughts came to me from beyond this earth. The presence of the thoughts came in the direction reaching from the Brilliance, Light, Darkness, Blackness and the Whiteness. The memories of those that know me are eternal

CHAPTER XXII

Prophesy to the presence of fear. Tell the people who know when to wait for a little while these words, "The yield of the fruit and the shaking of the earth bring the telling." Where do you see fear stand and wait for the unknown? The thing the earth fears is about the watch on the earth at each quaking of the earth. Heaven chose the throne and the quiet became to those watching who host the living thoughts. The moments beyond the fear came into the sight as the fear quieted. Before the fear came, the yield was known to be the fruits of the earth. The only thing lacking was that which knows to go away.

The height of the government of the United States of America has been in a great storm. The rain came as flashes from the reaching beyond this earth talking to each other. I watch the height of the government of America. I learned to see the same thing the police arouse called metro at their feelings. I wanted to teach this to the police. They refused to listen. I tried to bring about the instruction to the police by running for Sheriff.

The denial of the police pushed the seeking by the flashes from the stars beyond this earth to awaken only the return of God from the past. The flashes from the stars are thoughts. The people do not know how to think. The people recognize the thought passed from star to star. The people gather the thoughts and by their amazement, the people make believe they have the ability to think.

The name Jesus is the River of Life. God's name is eternity. You will know God in the name of God by the Return of God. I have put a hole in the police. The police are looking for a little Dutch boy to put his finger in the hole of the dam. I intend to find the little Dutch boy and by my finding him first, I can show him the view from the other side of the light called the darkness. The first thing he will see to do is put his finger in the Sheriff's gun barrel. The time he makes for his own race is to present the brilliance to stand beside the darkness. The Sheriff will need a double barrel six-gun with wiggly barrel ends to put his sight on the brilliance and the darkness in order to keep the progression only for the light.

When the blackness becomes to be the identity as the coming of the brilliance became to be the identity, the light and the darkness will be seen as this beginning becoming by the turn of the earth bringing the day and the night. High above the head between the morning and the evening is high noon becoming the distance to awakening from the north. This earth is following the northern star by the expansion present from the beginning by God all the way to eternity.

CHAPTER XXIII

The promise of life which is in the power of Christ Jesus granted these things by the word of God. The knowledge of God has been recognized. The formula of thought has been recognized. The child departs from the preparation of mankind on this earth. The way of the doctrine by mankind will only creep across the earth. I have sent that all I deliver out the mouth will be preserved in the written word. The cities have risen up. The court has become like a cork making the cities like a prison. Which of the many cities have been against me. I will pardon which have been against me, that I do them good.

Everything is remembered. Nothing is forgotten. Are there any people on this earth that can live in the awareness between the Alpha and Omega as it is revealed by these words I have been put to bring public?

The end time of the world of Jesus came at the end time of the year 2000. The Christ Jesus revealed the world of Jesus from the year one to the year 2000. The end time of the world of Jesus was foretold to come because the people wanted not the truth. The Christ Jesus appeared to me and put with me the answers to the world of Jesus. By this I have written there will be no denial in the world of Jesus and the world of Jesus will be completed.

The completing of the world of Jesus will bring about the completing of the world of God. Jesus was put to bring about the completing of the world of God. The people wanted not the truth. Jesus was taken away. Jesus promised to return and bring about the world of Jesus with the awakening of this side of this earth to the time before Adam. This awareness is written and will be brought public as foretold in the New Testament Revelation put public as desired by Jesus.

The world is by the cycle of 2000 years made by this universe. The end time of the world is a Harvest Time. The cycle of the year is 365 days and nights. The relativity of God's knowledge reveals the knowledge of God is shaped like a funnel from the rim of universe to the funnel spout being one year. The end time of the year is a Harvest Time. The end of the world is a Harvest Time. The beginning of the new world is this becoming by the truth put with me. I will bring about a continuing around this earth. This becoming by my effort has begun. I suggest you read my writings.

I am looking for people recognizing the direction being put by my communication with the life beyond this earth. I have learned to see inside my head. I learned to focus the sight before my eyes with the sight inside my head. The matching was God's rewards and God's answers building the world of God. The New Testament has foretold this message received personally. I obeyed Jesus and I put the message public. 6-66 became a formula for gathering. The 666 became a formula for thought reaching to continue beyond this earth.

CHAPTER XXIV

The snowflakes form a crystal. Why is the law in question? The snow forms a crystal as each snowflake adheres to the other snowflakes falling to the ground. Each snowflake holds its form, yet the field of snow is one blanket. The individuality of the law and the snowflake are similar. The flame of a fire commits the opposite deed. Given the powers of the mind, the word of the law should be more like the snow. Where is the joy in the law? The lamp contains the fire.

I have begun to fight the law. I wanted to start at the police and reach to the Sheriff's office. From the Sheriff's office, I wanted to extend my fight to the Mayor's office.

This beginning brings the fight to the Mayor, Governor and the President. The government of the United States of America is divided into three parts. One is the city. One is the state. One is the nation.

The present language used by the United States Government is inferior. The present language bringing the information to the people has a double standard. Former President Bill Clinton silenced all congress of the United States with one word. The word was "is".

Former President Bill Clinton asked one question to the Congress. The question was, "What is your opinion of the word is?" I wrote to the Supreme Court and I told them that the word "is" is an issue. Law is an issue. The Supreme Court of the United States has failed to comment or ask questions.

The reason I am starting a fight with the law is to put the law to be awakened to the right of the newborn. I met the Great Spirit of the Indian Nation. The Great Spirit brought the truth becoming with the Christ Jesus to appear to me. I found the reason Jesus was put away was that the law became by the right of the first born.

The people on this earth have been fighting the people and their fight should be with the law. I am standing up as only one to begin this fight with the law. I have no intention to laugh at the police like Hollywood to start this fight. I can see the nun's habit, the black and white police car and I try not to laugh when I think of the television show, "My Mother, the Car". When I think of the police helicopter and the television show, "The Flying Nun" it is hard to hold back the laughter.

The Great Spirit brought me to recognize the beginning of the law. I have become with the answers to turn the law. I have seen the reaching past the turn of the law bringing about the fold of the law. I have spent the time needed to put the images to a language. The direction of this language is the destiny.

CHAPTER XXV

Their God and their good upon this earth were by the yield of the fruits of this earth. The throw and the throne became by the sending. The stretches between the throw and the throne became the building of the cities. The feet became the rule by the throne. The cities became by the rule made by the hands. What do you see by these answers?

People, I will hear from the disheartened and the feeble. The similarity to the restless sea has been seen as an attack. Because of the harvest to the world at the end time of the world, I will replace the sword with the sickle.

The attack has been at a time where women and treasures were young and anchored by strings from the military. This pain was about when the land was like an empty jar. Those who filled the jar with blood made laughter to rule over time and anger to be the burning desire building about the people.

Who remembers the purity made by gold? Who remembers the stillness of the cities, when all the cities slept at night? Was this stillness the treasure of the cities or is the treasure the hustle and bustle of today?

Return to the greatness without a fight for the words to be with a judgment and give among the awakening by their speaking. The stars shall be as angles called angels because the answers pass this earth and only by this turn; the coming is neither to fight nor to roar like a lion.

The young will have the day and the darkness as the same strength with no more evil by the sight before the eyes and the sight inside the head. Ye have offered me the even, therefore I came upon you not against the songs and praises with words first to understand the earth by the sight before the eyes and the day and the night.

The strength put to fight is like fire. The awakening of this strength is without the greatness, once the fire has swept across the forests and the prairies. Who remembers the forest before the fire? Who remembers the sword before the coming of the gun? The building about time was seen. The awakening of yesterday becomes by the word written. Where is the memory about the past brought by joy in the law?

I came upon you by addition. The name Adam has been solved. The name Adpm has been awakened and by this awakening, the given becomes an even to the light of the day and the darkness of the night.

LETTERS TO PRESIDENT BUSH, PUTIN, FOX AND VICE PRESIDENT CHENEY

President George W. Bush
White House
1600 Pennsylvania Ave, N.W.
Washington, DC 20500
Dear President Bush:

I am ready to begin publishing. I have written to you. I have hand carried over one million words I have written from my own mind to the Mayor's office in Las Vegas, Nevada. I have been ignored.

The Secret Service has stopped to see me. They keep reminding me that they are your protection. It seems as though they are expecting me to be angered because I am being ignored. They ask questions. They want no answer to their question to be able to encompass the whole sight of the question bringing the answer.

I study their questions and their statements as they study mine. I have begun to see more than has been publicly recognized. I have begun to see what President Johnson meant when he said, "America has a sick society." After the interview was over, I noticed the people doing the questioning were trying to do what the Calvary did minding about the psychology.

The police and I have been in a fight all my life because of this practice. I solved the practice and I turned it to go the other way. The turn became similar to learning to put the pain of a hangover to go the other way presenting a window to the reasoning of the race across this land. The view coming from the recognition of the light is only able to reveal less than half a world. Look at the struggle between the white people and the native people. Look at the answers coming to the native. Look at the answers coming to the White pilgrims. The answers reaching the minding of the people coming to this land called America had more than 2000 years of intelligence marching back and forth on the other side of this earth before reaching to this side of earth. I can see the cause. I can also see the answers.

I have studied the bottom. I listen to the black people talk about the oriental people being given everything. I see the black people struggle from slavery with nothing and no education. I see the oriental being the best that can reach across the ocean. The will to be free is the will to progress with limitations being restricted. It is the other way in their environment to maintain control. I see the distance between the practice before the oriental people came to this side of earth and the practice of the black people on this land called America. I see the uneducated and poor black people in the races and competition for jobs and a place beside the white people in equality.

I look at my people. I am native to this land. I am ready to stand up. I want you not to think I am feeling sorry for the black people by my observation. I am not siding with the black or the oriental. I am not intending to put myself in a competition with the white, black or oriental. I see the minding of the Calvary being taught to the people on all sides of this earth. I see the path to walk across this land for my people first.

I see no native being encouraged like Secretary of State Colin Powell or Secretary of Education Rod Paige by the black people. The steps of equality for the black people are by demand. I see no way bringing about this I want by demand like the black people have been forced to do. I see no way by threat or violence. What I see is the way bringing world trade to the Indian reservations first. It is my intent to go to the reservations and start building hotels.

Did you ever watch a dice game? Did you ever wonder where the name paradise came from? I plan to build a paradise on the Indian reservations. I wrote and told Ada Deer about my plan. She saw what the white people, doing the Calvary thing, let her see. The presence of double borders was not in her sight. I will not tell you all I am talking about. I will require payment for the sight I have learned to see. How does $50 million a year sound to you?

I claim to have learned more than you and present authority in the White House, State Capitals and the City Halls. I claim to have taken the Oval office away from President Bill Clinton in the psychology. I claim to have met the Oval office Spirit. I met the Great Spirit of the Indian nation. I found the Great Spirit of the Indian Nation and the Oval office Spirit and the Spirit of God's love are the same spirit.

My answers will bring me to take the Oval office away from you at the flesh. I have learned to communicate with life beyond this earth. I have received the answers and written the answers. The completion of the answers will bring about the building of a new world. The new world will be built by a new government designed to the sun inside out. All the steps have been recorded. I need only to add names and addresses.

The addition of names and addresses can come from all nations. This good news can begin all over the world at the same time bringing world peace. The addition must first be lead by a possible new religion. The new religion begins by a worship put to the reasoning bringing the continuing around this earth. Former President Nixon tried this reach to continue around earth. He made too many errors. First he tried to put business to be like it was in the beginning of America, lawless. The Chinese are not the same force as the Native American.

The law has been damaged between the nations. The truth must be brought first to set free the indecision. The only way left is to bring about a new religion in worship of the continuing of God around this earth as earth turns about its axis. The height of the language is with the word God. The height of the mind is at this same word. The first presence bringing the awareness is not the communication. The people on this earth have seen this presence and by trying to communicate the awareness in a language, they can only recognize the language is inferior to God's knowledge. I want to get paid for the answers, so I will stop telling, until the money comes.

I do not need the American government for the first two parts in my intent. First I want to take the Great White Way to Russia. Second I want to bring about another continuing between Spain and Mexico. The two reaches to continue around this earth will be like feet in walking and the turn of hands. To see this I am saying without the answers, you must first recognize the distance between the feet and the hands. The path for the feet knows good and evil. The Alpha and the Omega by this I am doing will prove the plateau and the wall to the next step are the Alpha and Omega able to bring the End Time of the world to be relative to the End Time of the year as a Harvest Time. The present religions are leading the people away from mankind and to mankind in confusion because the identity to mankind knows only from birth to death.

It does you no good to send the Secret Service to see me. I went to school. There is no reason for me to do anything wrong.

Look at it this way. I and you are invited to a birthday party for the Oval office. You came to my side of this earth and took all that was mine. I have no gift to bring to the party. What am I to do? Am I to take your gift away from you and give it to the Oval office? Why should I be like you?

I will start a party on the reservations inviting all the world and you will find your invitation as all the world looks at you to see what you will do. What gift will you bring to my party as I claim the Great Spirit and the spirit of the Oval office are the same spirit?

I look at you and I see the way to bring your heart beat to be my steps to the Oval office. I need not your breath to be the sail of my boat. I have awakened the darkness. I have solved the 666. You are a threat to your nation. I am no threat to you. If for any reason you have an untimely persuasion between life and death it is because you know not between life and death. Your mind is with the distance between birth and death. I am the only one on this earth that can save you from your own destruction. I am your salvation. I am the good thing about this earth. I bring the answers to rise up the people.

Why do you not want to rise up? Government is not eternal. What is beyond government is the River of Life. The beginning of government which you claim from the podium as your government is at the beginning. I bring walls to both sides of your government putting your government to become like a river bottom. There is no way you can stop me. I need only tell the truth.

Would you like to see me or maybe stand beside me as I go to the Mid East and single handedly stop the war in the Mid East? The reaching comes as soon as I earn enough money for a plane ticket and the picture for my passport. I will tell you each step if you and your heart beat are beside me.

I will tell you enough to stop you from setting your mind to bring the President's Cabinet to start circling the wagons. I will claim the end of the war comes not by peace in the desert areas. Peace as America see peace is behind the tree with the rifle waiting for the lone native. I want peace to be seen by the people of this world from another direction because there are not enough trees in the desert areas.

Look at the mother of all wars. She saw the kid speak out. She did not care what was said. She slapped his mouth. Revenge takes a build up. The forces against terror are looking for the immediate following as thought the end of the caravan was the Calvary. Look at a real government. Had the tail of the rattler been the Calvary, what could have occurred on this land? Would peace have been another thing?

I am putting this on my computer as an insight to my writing. I expect this I am telling to be like a volcano. As long as no one by my authority intends to do anything wrong, I will jump on the edges of the volcano to make the hot, molten lava shoot higher. Be not surprised if I bring it about that President Vicente Fox of Mexico and I are the two top people on this side of earth. I am seriously looking at an exodus taking a lot of Mexican people back to Mexico.

You can learn to follow my thinking. The thoughts come from beyond this earth. I became an obedience to receive and write the answers. The obedience to complete the answers is now about the soul. Writing the answers set the spirit and the deep free. I saw the answers by my receiving the answers set God free. This awareness coming from God is by addition. I found the awareness in the name between the name God and the name Adam. I solved the name Adam. The name Adam means to add the AM. The addition bringing the name Adpm to awaken between the additions brings about my vision.

The sight goes both ways. One way is the sight inside the head. Why are you afraid to learn to see the sight inside your head? The sight reveals the kingdom of God, once you learn to focus the two sides of the brain like you focus the two eyes in the front of your head. The truth I tell is called the future. The New Testament Revelation has been solved and turned to go the right way without the Dead Sea Scrolls. What the Dead Sea Scrolls may offer is to be between you and Israel. I know the truth. I claim this you and the Prime Minister of Israel find will become the next step to the religion of Israel. I can make it happen by the way I reveal the truth to the world.

I want you to know I am not threatening the United States of America or you. I want you to see this I am telling as the speaking of a man. The mother of all wars has slapped the mouths of the military and the governments on this earth from the beginning of war. Could it be the father of all wars is the rudder on the boat, not the bravest warrior?

Look at the great big white man and the little native woman. Look at the kid. Look at the fact telling about survival being the heaven of the creatures. Where is the presence about the turn? The turn becomes not by equality. Why does not the kid look at the race? I will once again need payment for the outcome to the question. Even the big black man heads to the top of the white race. Is it in the reasoning of the race to be this knowing the sperms and the knowing bringing the sperm to be white in all male offers more in answers than is publicly accepted?

The communication I have learned becomes from life beyond this earth to the sperms. The sperms are in an identity to the life beyond this earth. There is an eye for an eye. There are prisons because the people on this earth put their seeds into the rectum. The sperms are in an identity to life beyond this earth; this is a communication with life. The mind of the earth became naturally at the End Time of the year 2000 as it was foretold. The mind of this earth encompasses both the light and the darkness. The coming of the darkness has been solved.

I intend to bring this I know public. Please awaken to the good news bringing the Judgment Time to turn to be a path to success for the good. Bringing this I know public will begin in so many places at the same time, world peace will seem the outcome. The observation will prove that each place is a different beginning. Suddenly the people will awaken and find the direction passed the turn being of one mind called peace. Going back does not help.

The turn to all go the same way is of one mind. The knowledge of God is like a funnel. Peace is like a funnel spout. The people searching for peace do not want peace when it comes because the turn to go the same way does not last. The individual nations do not bring the law to the table. How can business survive without the presence of the awakening to the law becoming to form the way awakening the continuing of the direction recognized as being of one mind? Individually the presence of one mind is with the specific answers to build the big picture called being of one mind.

I claim to have taken the Oval office away from President Bill Clinton during his administration. I will prove it by taking one half of his office away from him in Harlem. The feeling comes to me to want me to stare across the room at him from my desk and tell on him. The law is after the fact as an example as by the same telling.

Who is watching the past Presidents in this freedom of America? The bottom tells on the top. The question at the bottom is who is policing the police? I want all 6 living Presidents to debate me. I want all 6 living Presidents to be aware of the first six in the formula 6-66 and be aware of the 666 as a formula for thought. I want all 6 living Presidents to tell me what they are doing, what they have done and what they intend to do or I will begin the progress to take one half of their offices away from them.

It is no secret how I will start to take away President Bill Clinton's key to his office. The public gave him the key. The public will give a copy to me. I need only begin a bounty hunting business going after the wayward police. The reaching is actually the first steps. The first steps are the heart beat of the presiding President George W. Bush. I have become aware of the Political Fence bringing the two- party system to be a single strand of barbwire. I see all this from the view you taught to the entire world. "Me First."

It is not my intent to tell you the specific answers because they come from the same place as the answers to complete the present government. The answers come from Down Below. The answers rise up the people. Your fear of losing control by my standing up is evident. I laugh each time you say, "This is my government." I ask to the face I see on the TV screen, "It's not our government anymore?" You tell me it is our government for 200 years. Now you turn on the church. I watched the religions get mad at you. State knows the separation between church and state better than the church. The state built the separation between church and state. Your turning on me will not bring me or mine to revenge. We all go forward All Time by All Knowing Allah; the All Knowing of God called the Return of God.

Sincerely,

s/martin bector
Martin Bector
President

President George W. Bush
The White House
1600 Pennsylvania Ave NW
Washington, DC 20500

Dear President Bush:

I invite all America to come to my new office being lead by the love of God. I have learned to awaken the spirit in the psychology. I had to take the Oval office away from President Bill Clinton in the psychology to bring the mind about the Oval office to be clean enough to receive from the knowledge of God.

I met the Great Spirit. I am the native to this land who came down the mountain to meet the Great Spirit. I found the Great Spirit and the Oval office spirit are the same spirit. I came to be awakened by both the spirit and the deep from the beginning with God. The awakening can be taught. The instructions have been received and written.

I have learned to put my mind to the Oval office and it is my intention to begin teaching this practice to all people who are good, all around this earth. I will instruct the people on this earth who are good, to learn to put their mind to the Oval office and turn from seeking God to learn to receive from God. The presence of God is awakened on this earth by bringing the addition from the past to awaken the present to the possibilities of becoming the future.

I recognize that you have never learned to put your mind to the Oval office. I can tell because you are constantly trying to be above me in the psychology. This is impossible. I am the nativity on this land. I can put my mind to the beginning of this side of this earth. You can only put your mind to the day the first pilgrim put foot on my land.

My first thought was to stand up and take the Oval office away from you. Why not? I have the answers. All I have to do is make the two-party system become a single strand of barbwire and begin adding other successful two-party systems to begin building a political fence. The answers bring the law to look lake a wire basket.

The government and the law present the law to work from the outside in and the government to work from the inside out. The fascination in the knowledge of God is by the All Knowing. The All Knowing is so impressed by God's knowledge; the All Knowing seldom gets the feeling to bring about the communication with the Black Holes.

The reason for the deep fascination by the All Knowing of God is because the people on this earth refuse to recognize the coming of God in the Whiteness, the Brilliance, the Light, the Darkness and the Blackness.

The meeting at the center of the cross called the wrist of the Arm of Geddon at the opening comes as all directions turn to go the same way. This turn is being of one mind. The reason the people do not obey God is because some people on this earth are trying to live in the turn. The turn brings the entrance to the way of God.

My second thought has come to consume my attention. The second thought is for me to stand up as the President of the United States of America from the bottom up. The present government goes from the top down. This becoming was from Up Above. I bring the answers from Down Below. The rising up of the people on this earth begins by the judgment time I bring to become on this earth. I bring the judgment time for the good to be the path to success.

I have solved the New Testament Revelation written in the Holy Bible. The number, the letter, the sound, the color, the form and the image are the 6 revelations. The formula 666 is a formula for thought. The formula 6-66 is a formula for gathering the people to receive, write and complete the answers sent from God. God's answers must be completed first before the answers from beyond this earth, knowing beyond God, will be in harmony with the addition from the beginning knowing God.

I am interested in finding if you want to start the legislation recognizing this rise up of the people one giant step forward. The present economy is built by the top. I bring the answers to build the economy of the top into a river of life. I bring the answers to build an economy for the middle class and build an economy for the bottom. The rising up of the people will be all the people. The economy of the rich and the economy of the poor will stand side by side. The bottom will be the top and the top will be the bottom is the uniting of the states to be the United States of America. The United Cities of America stand up to reach to the top.

I see all the treachery on this earth and I can recognize the beginnings. It seems to me that every problem begins because you are trying to conquer me. Look at the many ways you try to put your direction to overcome the nativity. All of the people on this earth could begin to reach with the continuing around this earth instead of trying to conquer the reasoning for the people to be on this side of earth from the other side of earth.

All of you are still trying to conquer me. Recognize the course of my thoughts. I had to beg my teacher for a "D", so I could graduate from high school. I would ask a question. The teacher would say, "That's deep" and begin to talk all around the answer. I opened the door to the sight inside the head. I found the sight goes both ways. The presidency is patterned after the sight. The presidency goes both ways. One way is the sight before the eyes. The other way is the sight inside the head. I was going to instruct this as an institution. I found because of the sin on this earth, I will not be able to bring enough people to desire to turn and go the other way to make it profitable.

I have been instructed to start the building of the new world by a new government designed to the sun inside out. I have received and written the new government and the new law similar to a wire basket and the new religion. I can take the crown of England by simply revealing the return of God and the purpose of the Kingdom. The continuing is around this earth. I bring the people to worship in this continuing of God around this earth. I bring the people to worship the sperms. I can turn the people in the Orient worshipping the dead to turn and go the other way.

I have recognized the All Knowing of God called Allah. The return of Allah brings the gathering of the people to build world peace on this earth. The people have been trying to live in the answers. The turn is from opium to opinion. The answers must be built on this earth. Receiving the answers sets God free. Writing the answers sets the spirit and the deep free. Completing the answers sets the soul free. The people with no desire to complete their answers have no reason to be on this earth. The truth is on this earth. I knew as a child. I just was not able to interpret the images into a language awakening the mind of this earth to the presence aware of the possibilities for the future.

Sincerely,

s/martin bector
Martin Bector
President

Vice President Richard Cheney
The White House
1600 Pennsylvania Avenue NW
Washington, DC 20500

Dear Vice President Cheney:

What is the way of life? I am not trying to point you a path by my question. I want only to bring from the heart and mind of the American people the same pulse.

I found a relationship with the thought bringing a presence from the heart. I recognized the pulse of the blood could awaken the mind to a one minding. All people can recognize this pulse. All people can become of this one mind. Being of one mind awakened by the pulse of the heart beat is individual with all people and at the same time this pulse brings all people to be of one mind.

The way of life is this recognition of the pulse of the blood at the brain. The way is this same path put to a chart bringing the diagram of a circle to be the same as the course this solar system makes as it travels through the sky. The path and the pulse of the blood bring about relativity. The mind has been solved.

The End Time of the Year took away the forgiveness and the reaching from the darkness became to reveal all that has been denied. The darkness does not know the people. The darkness knows the mind of this earth as the light knows the mind of this earth. The reaching is to the presence from the nativity. I am the oldest ancestry of this earth being on this side of earth. The passing away of the forgiveness awakened the beginning of a new world.

I have no problem with the present government at the flesh. The people trying to conquer this side of earth are all with the White House with their will against me. I care not because the will has no life. The jungle creatures did not find this side of earth like they found the other side of earth. The presence of America trying to follow England brings only the fear from Africa. Grow up the minding of American to a better plateau. It is your job as the Vice President. Yes you can say that I am telling on you and telling you what to do at the same time. We are about the same age.

I do not feel like the white people or the black people about the height of the office. The tree ring is the ripple and the tree sap is the raindrop. The leaves are the crown. The kingdom of the forest is not the same as the kingdom of the flat lands. Even the turn of the water on the mountain is going only one way.

I am native to this land. I have begun to take over the tribes. I claim to be the Big Bear of the Mountain Tribes. I will gather my people. I have two offerings, one is the nativity politic and the other is a political fence. I will start these two progressions at the universities. It may be wise to get the Secretary of Education in a corner and whisper a few chosen words bringing him to look at my website.

I feel like the White House is Junior High. I have learned to put my awareness from the brilliant stars all the way to the black holes. The revealing brings visions to be all about the direction of my sight. The study of the visions brought me to learn to interpret the images. The Wisemen learned this same interpretation and the becoming from the interpretations came the word of God.

I have brought the interpretation from the beginning and from the presence. The meeting came bringing visions. The reaching was free from the insult by the sin of Adam. The reaching became from beyond the time of Adam. The insult by the people still trying to conquer this side of earth has come to their end Time. The insult turned into tears and the interpretation came with the answers to build a new world.

I will begin building this new world by bringing the people on this earth a new government designed to the sun inside out. The new law is similar to a wire basket. The politic of the two party system will look like a single strand of barbwire. I intend to build the political fence. I wrote to Governor Jeb Bush. I intend to put a Cuban and Mexican two party system together. I would like the participation of Castro. I want both President Fox and President Ponce de Leone to participate.

I am not looking for agreement. The finish could address this testing. I am looking for the places to begin to build the fence posts. The political fence can become like latitude and longitude lines. The law similar to a wire basket can benefit by the fence posts the most. The fence post will be kept secret by the request put by Jesus in the Holy Bible. The reason is the people will want to bring the fence post to be the entire politic. The instructions bring the joy of the law and the entity to be a brand new happiness.

Keeping the secret will bring the political parties to come with the awareness knowing the joy in the law. The presence of the police knows not the law or its reason. The police are trying to live in the joy of the community minding. I intend to put the mind free from the present practice used by the police to try and control the people.

I have started a communication with Dr. Rice and many people working the governments of many nations. I intend to bring the great white way to Russia. I am by the opinion that former President Nixon made an error in judgment. I want to right another wrong. I have received and written the answers to bring a loan of $100,000 to every Mexican citizen. The exodus to Mexico will expose many ways to begin filling the empty jobs. It may be a good time to study the effect of the exodus and prepare. Every Mexican will be in a middle class status all in one giant step forward.

The secret is soon to come more public. I have studied the bottom and I can create the practices that will put the Mexican money to great works all across both sides of this earth. The publicity will make me famous, also being both a good artist and writer; I intend to get very rich. I intend to go to the Mideast and put an end to the war. I want Palestine to become a state in the United States for a short time. The people could pay the cost back, once the establishing of the support for the foundation of a state is built.

The younger people can begin to question the direction of the state of Palestine, once the state of Palestine becomes a state of Israel. The meeting of the youth and the elders is the first agreement to bring peace to the

Middle East. Gathering the agreements begins the national peace between Palestine and Israel and one day or night there could be peace all over the world for ever and ever.

Sincerely,

s/martin bector
Martin Bector
President

Vice President Richard Cheney
The White House
1600 Pennsylvania Avenue NW
Washington, DC 20500

Dear Vice President Cheney:

Please look at my website while it is innocent and beginning. I have begun to learn the basics about computer technology. My assistant, Ray Bergman, built this website by my instruction concerning the material on my website. I am reaching to bring a communication between my office and the Oval office. I deem this necessary because I have learned to communicate with life beyond this earth. Some are not friendly to the denial. Others are more patient.

The life beyond this earth taught me this I know. It is very possible the life beyond this earth is tired of the constant delay in completing the answers that bring God's answers needing completion. The need for this completion is to know the harmony between the reaching from God, the reaching from beyond God and the reaching from following God. Teaching other things could reach others.

The presence beside God is called the All Knowing of God. The presence of Allaha and the return of Allaha becomes at the presence becoming as God and the presence becoming as the return of God. The presence of mind is this knowing the coming of God.

The sight goes two ways. One way is this sight before the eyes. The other way is the sight inside the head. God put the miracle of dreams to reveal the sight inside the head. The sight inside the head is the Kingdom of God. The sight before the eyes is the River of Life. The government is not eternal. The answers have been readied to bring the government to become a river bottom. The day and the night are in the identity to each a knowledge from before mankind came to this earth by the way of the language. The day is in the identity to a language. The night is in an identity to a language. The identity has been raised out of the wilderness by reading the words I write.

I want this not to be a religion or a government. I want this business to yield $25 a page and progress through the books to the chapters at $25 a chapter. No one will be stopped at paying me $25 a paragraph. The people in this participation can also begin by paying $25 for each sentence and another $25 for each word or individually putting one or two beginnings.

The $25 charge is for this one "Book of Poems" by Martin Bector. I will let each participant borrow $200 at the 12th participant. Pay the loan and receive 10 time each loan.

Here is a sample of how the formula 12 program would work:

FORMULA 12 PROGRAM		
AMOUNT OF LOAN	**PAYBACK AT 12**[TH] **PARTICIPANT**	**ELIGIBLE TO BORROW**
$200	$200	$2,000
$2,000	$2,000	$20,000
$20,000	$20,000	$200,000
$200,000	$200,000	$2,000,000
$2,000,000	$2,000,000	$20,000,000

Sincerely,

s/martin bector
Martin Bector
President

81

President Vicente Fox
Los Pinos
México D.F.
MÉXICO

Dear President Vicente Fox:

I have begun to bring public this study I have been working on to a beginning from the ancestry on this side of the earth. The people coming over to this side of this earth from the other side have brought this knowing their ancestry on the other side of this earth. The conflict between the people on this side of this earth has not been solved because the ancestry from the other side of this earth has no way to know the answers knowing this side of this earth from the beginning.

The people on this side of this earth are not lost to God. The people on this side of this earth have lost the answers awakening the truth from the beginning. The awakening is called the Harvest Time. Only one needs to stand up on this side of this earth because there was only one color of people on this side of the earth.

I have written to you and told you that I have taken over Mexico. Mexico is not offended. I can walk the streets of Mexico all alone, day or night. I have asked you to surrender to me the Mexican Mafia. I did not tell you why because I wanted to make sure there was a public distance between your political achievements and the underworld like the Mafia. The idea in itself put the sight to see the necessary answers. I need to clean the Mexican Mafia up. I have begun a request to Spain to bring the value of the gold stolen from Mexico, in the past, back to Mexico as a gigantic loan making every ancestry in Mexico rich. The truth can be this by the name held dear by the Mexican people to be the similarity to the linage held dear by the Jewish people. The money can come to both the ancestry to Spain and the ancestry to the land of Mexico as a check and balance.

I have seen the answers to turn the Mexican Mafia into a Banking System. The great amount of money will be a loan. I have received the answers to bring the Mexican people to pay back the loan making Spain rich at the pay back. The greater the registration the greater the loan. I want to bring all the people out of the hiding places to do the registration for the rewarding. I want the Mexican Mafia to clean up the people hiding. By this process of cleaning it is like the left hand helping wash the right hand.

The people who have been scavengers in the dumps and the alleys will become rich. The schools that can teach these people to be good at the citizenry about the money making money as the next Salvation following the reward. The instructions have to be put into the development bringing this fortune back to Mexico must be received in a way to strengthen every cell in the Mexican Government as a body governing the people of Mexico.

I am preparing the people on this side of the border for a rising up into a river of life at the top. I am instructed to start at the top and the bottom at the same time. I am instructed to start at both sides of the borders at the same time to create a foundation each side can stand on going deeper from the border all the way to the Office of the President on both sides of the border. This foundation and this teaching must be built. Prayer is not the answer to this continuing awakening to the answers this earth passes through like the wind.

Sincerely,

s/martin bector
Martin Bector

President Vicente Fox
Los Pinos
Mexico D.F.
MEXICO

Dear President Fox:

The time has come. I saw in my mind a wrist with a wrist watch. I could not find the following about the time. I sat still. Another wrist with a watch appeared. The second wrist was farther away seeming smaller.

I can not wait any longer. I must stand up and begin at the Four Corners. This beginning is the New Testament Revelation. I have begun assimilation at the Main Gate of Nellis Air Force Base in Nevada. I want to bring a little revelation to the main gate at Nellis Air Force Base and a larger revelation to the Four Corners beginning in Colorado.

I know this awakening after reading the Holy Bible and the reaching to me from the Great Spirit. The Great Spirit and the Oval Office Spirit are the same Spirit. The view of the Spirit from the Night Time awakens by the void first and adds the AM is a commandment to add the AM. The presence of the Deep brings the commandment to add the PM. The name Adpm has been awakened to the mind of this earth.

I am interested in putting a New Testament Revelation in every nation on this earth. I solved the New Testament Revelation. There are 6 revelations. The first two, number and letter are this bringing two in one to be the first steps. The relativity in the knowledge of God presents the Light and the Darkness. This awareness begins at the Brilliance. The registration is with the Brilliance. Gathering is with the Light. The reach to gather at the center of the Cross from the four ends of the Cross is the New Testament Revelation. All turning to go the same way is being of one mind at the turn.

The turn and the salvation are not the same. The turn is with the answers to bring about the turn. The salvation is the money to complete the answers bringing about the turn. The money is the value of the wealth taken from Mexico. The wealth taken to Spain can return as a loan able to be paid back to Spain with an interest making all the people in Spain rich. The great amount of money loaned to Mexico can make all Mexico rich.

The continuing around this earth is this becoming from the answers I received coming to the presence about this worship I have developed bringing about the continuing of God around this earth. The answers bring the cleaning of the bottom. The people who are presently rich will come to build a River of Life out of their present economy. The cleaning of the bottom will bring to be built an economy for the bottom. The present concern is to build an economy for the middle class. Mexico has a strong top. President Ponce de Leon has a 72 year politic as a pillar of strength. The work you are doing begins a politic for the bottom. The money I am bringing to Mexico will be divided between the rich and poor evenly. Other decisions must be brought public and decided on democratically, so there is no disagreement leading to a thing unwanted.

I see the way to begin with wages from employment to gather pledges and begin instructions preparing the people for the coming of the money. The money should be at least $100,000 for every person in Mexico before the cut off date. The babies born after the cut off date will be even more rewarded. The turn will bring each new born to be like a king.

The return payment to Spain plus interest will bring every person in Spain to be rich. The wealth can come to every one like a reverse tax in Spain or in lump sums like a lottery. The use of both at the same time puts levels able to bring the people who are good to want to be better. All people will have to be good to receive the reaches to riches.

The death of Jesus has been solved. The law and the right put for the first born put the people to bring an end to the real truth. The presence of Jesus appears to me with these answers revealed to me the truth comes with the new born. The Spirit knowing mankind as the male first and the feelings knowing woman first became awakened by the presence of the Deep knowing the Night Time first.

Sincerely,

s/martin bector
Martin Bector

President Vladimir Putin
Russian Federation
Russia, Moscow
Kremlin, 103073

Dear President Putin:

The tiny little snowflakes never kiss until the touch the ground. The thoughts of mankind have this relativity. Mankind has errors by thinking mankind can think. The thoughts come from beyond this earth. Image in the mind is this presence.

The people on this earth have been forced to try to live in the recall. The recall is this reach inside the brain to the memory. It is like the people are trying to put life inside out.

I want you to join me to bring the people life becoming with the people reaching from beyond this earth. I want not this to be with the present religions. I bring the coming of the light called the return. The reach to this side of this earth can continue around this earth to the other side of this earth.

The presence of this earth has a mind. The people on this earth have put their mind to be in identity to the day and the night. The outcome brings the white people and the black people to take turns following each other.

This earth turns about its axis. The continuing of God is with this earth. In the present identity with mankind on this earth you must bring the Russian people to protect their night blessings being the next step to the day blessings. The night time is down below to the day time on the other side of this earth.

It would be better if the Russian people learned to recognize the light as the first step and the darkness as the next step when eyes are closed. The Holy Bible prepared the people on this earth for the turn from the sight before the eyes to the sight inside the head. By learning to bring the Miracle of Dreams to reveal the sight inside the head, the mind need not be forced to try and penetrate the identity becoming about mankind as the source of thought. The identity put to mankind knows only from birth to death. The identity to the past can only lead the people backwards.

I am interested in helping you bring Russia to reach all around this earth. The prophet recognized the answers from the spirit. The profit brings the flesh to comfort the soul. I want to propose the reach to Russia from America. I have recognized the attempt of former President Nixon to take the Great White Way to China was an error. The Great White Way is this continuing of God around this earth. The reach of the Great White Way should reach Russia from the United States of America.

I have begun to develop a new export and import system able to stand beside the present system. I would like to bring the new system to be like a wire bundle with a red carpet from every door to city hall. The government is city, state and nation.

I would appreciate an invitation and you're considering my request to bring the Great White Way to Russia and also to publish in Russia. I am also interested in bringing a new religion to Russia bringing the continuing around this earth. Like snowflakes, the old system and the new system need not kiss. Standing side by side both systems can be like the feet in walking or the hands in movement.

Sincerely,

/s/Martin Bector
Martin Bector
President

President Vladimir Putin
Russian Federation
Russia, Moscow
Kremlin, 103073

Dear President Putin:

I am ready to begin the communication I have written to you explaining the Harvest of the World brought about by the turn of the New Testament Revelation to go the right way. I had to become the 666 in order to see the truth.

It was really simple. I like the way the Russian government made the Russian writers put a happy ending on all the writings brought public. Russia's belief that God is good and the position of the Government should help and God brought me to the first clue in solving the New Testament Revelation.

I have brought the 666 from the gathering for a great war to become a gathering of the like minded people to progress their intelligence and ability. I began with the turn from the 666 to the 6-66 as a formula. The formula 6-66 is this reaching from the north to the center of the cross in the MidEast. The 6-66 is a formula for one side of this earth. The meeting of the two sides of this earth brings the formula 12. The reasoning for the formula 12 is the same bringing the 12 months to the Year.

I know it is hard to change the habits of the people. This is the reason I want to bring the Russian Mafia to become a Politic. In this way the present Politic of Russia can be like the step of the right foot and the new Russian Mafia Politic can be the step of the left foot bringing Russia to go forward in the same direction like walking or running. This awakening can bring the distance between the steps to be the Destiny.

I will remind you again the Communism being by two influences; one knowing need to be in harmony with China and the other to find a way to combat the wealth of the White brought about by slavery of the Black people has become at the same wall to the next step called the End Time of the Year 2000.

I want to start a business bringing the Great White Way from the United States of America to Russia. The Spirit of both Russia and America find the needed peace between the two nations. The business is a profit business. The government, religion, law and society are non-profit. The way of God begins as non-profit at the gathering. This became in the beginning because the army was the best way to bring about the communication in the past. The people saw not this ability of the army and to this Day and Night, the people have not recognized this ability of the military.

The business I intend begins by my charging $25.00 a page for my writing. I bring the money to one hub. I loan $200.00 to the 12 participants filling up the pyramid of names by starting at the 6th participant in small areas. In the larger areas, I use 10 participants to gather the $200.00. Two participants bring about the profit used for expenses, salaries and profit. Government can tax both the $200.00 and the $50.00.

The beginning is so simple. Rising up the people by area saturation reaches to the next step in the Way of God. The Way of God is gathering, measuring, employment and freedom. The reach to Freedom first was brought about by the Christ Jesus because there was slavery. There never has been slavery in Russia. This turn from slavery is the cause bringing about the problem where there never has been slavery. Russia needs this truth to find freedom.

I will tell only one step at a time to make sure I get the credit and the profit I need to bring about this business. I am native to the land called the United States of America. I have been left out by the people in America and I have learned to leave gaps, to ensure I am not left out again.

I enjoy writing to you because the mind is more free by my writing to you than by my writing to President George W. Bush. It is like a breath of freshness sweeping across my mind. I credit this feeling to the fact of the night blessings of Russia knowing this about the continuing of God around this Earth.

I am ready to purchase a cell phone. If you send to me a phone number, I will call you and bring to you more detail promoting the Great White Way reaching from America to Russia. I saw the meeting on television of you and President George W. Bush at Crawford, Texas. I was impressed and I noticed how comfortable President George W. Bush was by being by your side. I like that sight and it would be great if all Americans felt as comfortable about Russia.

Sincerely,

s/martin bector
Martin Bector
President

President Vladimir Putin
Russian Federation
Russia, Moscow
Kremlin, 103073

Dear President Putin:

I became by the death of the one the Republican Party would give up to in the psychology to recognize the continuing around this earth. The recognition brought the world to be this now called the Public Mind. The mind can be put to be with the day and the night like a mirror to reveal the two sides of this earth and echo the awareness.

I learned to recognize the sight inside my head. The sight goes both ways. One way is the sight before the eyes. The other way is the sight inside the head. The presidency is patterned after the sight before the eyes. The sight inside the head is the kingdom of God. God put the miracle of dreams to reveal the sight inside the head.

I have learned to communicate with life beyond this earth. The communication becomes to the sperms by simply knowing. The sight inside the head is this called feelings by the women because the women have no sperms. The sperms are white in all male. The oriental people have been in the happiness searching for the River of Life. The River of Life is this becoming to Russia as the Great White Way.

I need no government to begin this business bringing the Great White Way. I am writing to you to ask you to become President of the Black Belt Organization similar to the National Guard able to reach to a place and leave just as sudden and as thorough. President Bush heads up both the Republican and Democratic parties, you can head up both the Black Belt Organization and the Russian Federation. The world wide Black Belt organization will use body power to push the peace and separate the resistance by an over population saturation. Hundreds on a free vacation for a few hours or a few days is much better than the way of proposing present help in disagreements and agreements.

The death of the person about the height of the psychology put me to be the big bear of the Indian Nation. I will begin to build cities on the reservations. I will spark up the Indian American Nations. I am interested in using the tribes about the reservations as cleaning stations across this nation for the preserving of the beauty of the Great White Way.

I am bringing a lot of money to Mexico. I want you to be in one of the first lines to bring about a giant loan from Mexico to Russia. I will put the money to be divided between the top and the bottom. Both the top and the bottom can loan out the money. Your government can borrow and each individual can also borrow from other individuals. With the computer, accuracy and speed, so many things can be progressed. The money going to Mexico City alone is more than $800 billion. The money comes from the wealth taken from Mexico. The wealth is not returned. The value is put to be loaned to the nation Mexico.

The answers came to me to bring the Mexican people to pay back the money and build a new world. The profit from building and selling the new businesses and manufacturing and selling the product pay the loan.

Sincerely,

s/martin bector

President Vladimir Putin
Russian Federation
Russia, Moscow
Kremlin, 103073

Dear President Putin:

Day and Night were put about this earth before the coming of the vegetation, the creatures and mankind. Before the names were put to the identity becoming Day and Night, the Light and the Darkness were these things about the truth. I am not saying that the Day and the Night are not the truth. I am telling that the Day and the Night are the first words God gave to the people on this earth.

Communication is this about the mind awakening between the people on this earth. I have learned a communication reaching to this earth from before the coming of God to the black hole called a void in the Holy Bible. This awareness was foretold in the New Testament Revelation to be on this earth at the End Time of the year 2000.

The present form of communication between the people on this earth has been in the acceptance of the Light as the sight before the eyes. The sight goes both ways. One way is the sight before the eyes. The other way is the sight inside the head. God put the miracle of dreams to reveal the sight inside the head. The denial to God has been solved.

I have learned to communicate with the void before the coming of God to this universe. The people on this earth have not wanted the truth. The people on this earth in the majority want only the awareness bringing the coming of God in the Light. The communication becoming to me from beyond God reveals the coming of God in the Whiteness, the Brilliance, the Light, the Darkness and the Blackness.

The communication reaching from the black hole before the coming of God puts the Whiteness, Brilliance, Light, Darkness and Blackness as this awareness in identity to the number of the extensions beyond the palm of the hand recognized as the fingers and the thumb.

This awareness has been recognized as the right hand of God. This awareness to your side of this earth has been called good. The awareness to my side of this earth has been called evil. The left hand of God has been solved. This earth turns about its axis. The morning horizon and the evening horizon are the same reaching from the east as this earth turns bringing the sun to appear to rise up in the morning and set in the evening.

The religions have put confusion about the government by calling the Light as good and the Darkness as evil. The Light on your side of this earth becomes the same evil in the Darkness. The truth continues around this earth by the answers reaching from God in the Light and from the black hole in the Darkness.

I have gone to school. I learned the history of the people on your side of this earth. I recognized that the governments and the religions became by area separations. Had the people on your side of this earth recognized the continuing around this earth, religion would have been another thing. I recognized that the people in the government of Russia in the past tried to bring about this awareness. The confusion brought about by religion was recognized by the people in Russia.

The governing begins at the economy. I have recognized the step between Communism and Capitalism. I recognized the reason of

Communism. I have recognized the reason of Democracy. The Russian people had no slaves. The people in the north of the United States of America found the long winters used up the slave money. The United States had a choice to stop the slavery or separate the North and the South.

The Southerners went to the North and bragged about their wealth. The North could not compete with the slave money as the Russians could not compete with the slave money in the World Market. Russia turned to Communism to bring about the gathering needed to compete with the slave money. Because of lack of the needed communication to see the problems and solve the problems, Russia and America did not recognize the continuing around this earth was the answer.

I have no intention to awaken the fight between the people recognizing the areas of religion and the areas of government. I am not interested in bringing changes to either Russia or to America. I am interested in bringing the World Market to the reservations in the United States. I am not with the people on the reservations being called Indians. I am the oldest ancestry of native on this land. I see the name Indian to be this awakening to the presence knowing the Heaven of the nation on your side of this earth named India.

The continuing around this earth has been recognized and by this awareness, the truth opens to find a clear mind at the name native rather than the name Indian. The name native lets the identity become to awaken the nativity about all lands. I am interested in bringing about a nativity as a politic able to continue around this earth. This I envision is not a world government. This I envision is a world politic.

I am interested in bringing to the United States a political fence. I am bringing the American people to awaken to this fact putting the two party system in the United States to be a single strand of barbwire. The addition of many strands of barbwire will complete the political fence. I intend to keep the fence posts a secret, until the strands of barbwire are formed, recognized and publicly accepted.

The people on this earth are confused by the Religions and this confusion has been solved. I expect to gather large sums of money for the answers reaching to this earth from the black hole called the void and other black holes. The confusion of the religions brought the people to try to identify with the Day and the Night as an identity to the people, not the language. The identity to the presence of mankind on this earth knows only from birth to death.

I would like to bring to your attention the belief of the oriental people and the belief of the Jewish people. The people by the Jewish religion try to put the identity to the linage of Adam. One line of the aged is this called a linage. The Oriental people recognize not the single reaching from the star called the eastern star. The Oriental people put the line being this reaching from the cluster of stars called a ling. The American flag is about this cluster of stars, yet in the confusion because of the present religions.

Sincerely,

s/martin bector
Martin Bector
President

President Vladimir Putin
Russian Federation
Russia, Moscow
Kremlin, 103073

Dear President Putin:

The universe has been solved. Russia won the Miss Universe contest. The cycle of this universe is every 2000 years. The New Testament Revelation foretold this End Time was a Harvest of the World. Our friends, the Jew put the message personal and turned the public awareness away from the office and put the sight before the eyes to the person elected to office.

The Jew's answers have been recognized and put public. The exodus of the Jew from Russia stopped the problem enough for me to solve the continuing around this earth. I have taken over the Russian mafia. I intend to bring the Great White Way to Russia free from the presence of unwanted. The Russian mafia will bring the Great White Way from America to Russia.

The Russian mafia will become a politic. The Russian mafia will begin the political fence in Russia. I have brought the awakening of the reaching power and the reaching force to turn the two party system in the United States of America in to a single strand of barbwire. The barbs keep the political lines in order. The barbs become the legislation. The law I have received and written is similar to a wire basket. The present law has only built city sprawl looking like the bottom of a wire basket.

I will keep the turns in the law and the folds in the law a secret from the United States of America to bring about the fold of the law as the return of God reaching around this earth. This awakening reaching from Russia to the people in America will bring about the replacement of the United States Congress by a computer. I will start at replacing the City Council in the city of Las Vegas, Nevada with a computer. Going forward is the presence of progress. Going forward is the message the people coming to my side of this earth used to take from me, this land, and all the wealth that is on this side of this earth.

The voices of America will be stopped by killing the retarded. The mindlessness of the retarded have not the sense to tell the truth. The presence of God from the beginning is by addition. The truth is from the beginning all the way to eternity before the coming of mankind to this earth.

The exodus of the Muslims should have followed the exodus of the Jew. The American people putting the Muslim to replace the Jew in the insult to the continuing around this earth can be put to rest before the insult becomes to bring a cold war to the two sides of this earth. I am suggesting all the

Muslims go to Palestine and bring back the balance that was destroyed by the error made by the Carter administration forcing the End Time to be a death of the world instead of a harvest of the world.

I found the government of the people in Yugoslavia was built by the World Banking System to be like a trampoline. The direction of the United States knows not the practice of building governments. The identity to the government of the United States of America is in the shape of a funnel. I offered to bring about a government for the troubled Middle East and the United States began to increase the minding put against me by the collective minds of the police, fire department and city hall. It is my opinion, America knows the reasoning of the past and I intend to bring the truth to the people on this earth.

I am in a communication with the life beyond this earth. I am ready to go the reservations, build cities on the reservations and bring about a World Market to every reservation. The mayor of Las Vegas, Nevada is a Jew. The governor of Nevada is a Catholic. The President of the United States is a Christian. The way by the governing of these three will become to be this assembling to gather as the fourth. Before the end of these three terms, I intend to bring a meeting of the four assemblies to meet at the center of the cross as foretold in the New Testament Revelation to become at the End Time of the year 2000.

I intend to go to the reservations to teach this I know. All the people on this earth will be invited to come to the reservations to learn the truth becoming awakening to the knowledge of God shaped like a funnel passing this earth. The Jew put the Passover to keep the Passover revealing the knowledge of God passes this earth. The Jew forgot what his daddy had in mind. I found the answers lost to the people on this earth. I intend to put a charge to every person on this earth for these answers. I intend to be the richest man on this earth in a few months. There is nothing anyone can do to stop me.

I bring the law to recognize the new born. The present law recognizes the first born in the interpretation of the law. The joy in the law has been found. I will bring this joy in the law to reveal the turn from control by the law to a harmony by the law bringing about the way of God to the people on this earth. The answers bring the way of God to build a new world for God. The new world is built by a new government I have received and written designed to the sun inside out. The present governments are able to be a foundation for the new government.

I have asked the First Lady of Nevada to find an interest in being the President of the United Cities of Nevada. I intend to bring about the United Cities of America as the next step to the United States of America. The United Cities of America will request a seat on the President's Cabinet in

America to stand side by side the United States making America even stronger. I want to check and balance this strength with the continuing around this earth brought from America to Russia by the Russian mafia.

I have asked President George W. Bush's government to bring Palestine to be a state in the United States of America for a time long enough to build a state about Palestine able to be recognized by Israel. I have been refused and ignored. I am turning to Russia to bring about this progress bringing Palestine to be a state in the Federation of Russia, until the state of Palestine is able to be recognized by Israel.

I am standing up as the Big Bear of the Mountain Tribes. I have met the Great Spirit. I have gone to school. I am ready to bring the presence of this side of earth to reveal the time before Adam and the time following Adam to the people on this earth. The continuing around this earth will be put public. I want to teach you and all Russia how to put your mind to the Oval office in the United States of America. I want to build an Oval office for North Korea to begin the following step in the progress coming from the new worship bringing the continuing of God.

Sincerely,

s/martin bector
Martin Bector

President Vladimir Putin
Russian Federation
Russia, Moscow
Kremlin, 103073

Dear President Putin:

There will be a place for peace in the Night Blessings of Russia. I have learned to protect the Night Blessings of Russia that were being insulted in the Darkness of this side of this earth.

The protection brought the Night Blessings to reveal the same truth as the mind of the Russian people awakened to every morning. I have begun by 30 years of practice to recognize the Heaven of Russia. I was put up to this in secret by the words written in the Holy Bible.

I am bringing the continuing of God around this earth. The Great White Way will reach from America to Russia. There will be a place in the continuing recognized by the government where you and I can fight for the decisions in an arena. We will both see one goal. At one place we will turn to go the same way or we will fight. You aren't threatened by this encountering of words as President George W. Bush Jr. is threatened if I approach him with the same statement. Black belt has a more awakened mind to the strengthened conversations of men.

Be amazed as I tell you the tongue of the Dragon has become a red carpet from every door to the city hall. The United Cities will become to stand after slaying the dragon as a strength to be added to the new course of the United States. One and one is two. Power and power is force. The United Cities will only make the United States stronger.

I am ready to go to the reservations and spark up the nativity. You may be interested in having the shadows of the rocks bring to Russia many secrets before they become secrets by a helping hand.

Sincerely,

s/martin bector
Martin Bector
President

AUTHOR'S NOTE

Thanking you for reading this little book are the Little Kids in Outer Space and Myself, Martin Bector

The dedication of this book is to the Little Kids in Outer Space, whom I have learned to communicate with. The reaching of this dedication by the Little Kids in Outer Space is with the knowing where everything has life.

ABOUT THE AUTHOR

Martin learned wild and forests knowing the love of creatures. The things about the wilderness awakened steps, where love awakens feelings. Martin grew up in Caldwell, Idaho. The cowboys and he became friends after a fight. Sometime he wondered if the fight was not the thing that moved this great nation forward.

Martin is native to this land and he sometimes refrains from calling himself an Indian because he can see the presence becoming the heaven of India in the continuing around this earth in the name Indian. He put the light and the darkness to be like the building of a mirror. Martin found he could awaken by this reflection the heaven of the other side of this earth in the continuing around this earth.

He was born in Mona Vista, Colorado in 1939 and at the age of thirty-three met the Great Spirit of the Indian Nation. He learned the Great Spirit of the Indian Nation and the spirit of the Oval office are the same spirit as the love of God.

Martin did a pilgrimage across America from coast to coast and border to border.

www.ingramcontent.com/pod-product-compliance
Lightning Source LLC
Chambersburg PA
CBHW030359290526
45785CB00004B/1817